Released 1984

THE TASTE OF OUR TIME

Collection planned and directed by

ALBERT SKIRA

BIOGRAPHICAL AND CRITICAL STUDY

BY

PIERRE GASSIER

Translated by James Emmons

GOYA

SKIRA

Title Page:
Portrait of the Duchess of Alba (detail), 1795.
Collection of the Duke of Alba, Madrid.

Published by Skira Inc., Publishers, New York, N.Y.

Library of Congress Catalog Card Number: 55-10594.

CHRONOLOGICAL SURVEY

1746 Birth on March 30, at Fuendetodos (province of Saragossa), of Francisco de Paula José Goya, son of José Goya, a master gilder, and Doña Gracia Lucientes.

1746 Birth of Ramón Bayeu and Luis Paret.

1748 Birth of David.

1752 Founding of the Royal Academy of Fine Arts of San Fernando, Madrid. Louis-Michel Van Loo leaves Madrid and returns to France.

1753 Corrado Giaquinto paints ceiling frescos in the Royal Palace, Madrid. Birth of Agustín Esteve.

1755 Birth of John Flaxman.

1757 Birth of William Blake.

1760 Goya begins a four years' apprenticeship in the studio of José Luzán at Saragossa.

1761 Anton Raphael Mengs comes to Madrid.

1762 Giovanni Battista Tiepolo comes to Madrid.

1763 Though barely seventeen, Goya competes for a scholarship at the Academy of San Fernando, Madrid, but fails.

1764 Death of Hogarth. Winckelmann publishes his "History of Ancient Art."

1766 Goya again competes for a scholarship at the Academy of San Fernando, again fails.

1766 Death of Nattier.

1768 Death of Canaletto.

1769 Birth of Thomas Lawrence.

1770 Goya goes to Italy.

1770 Death of G. B. Tiepolo in Madrid. Death of Boucher.

1771 Goya awarded second prize in a competition at the Royal Academy of Fine Arts, Parma. Back in Spain, he receives his first commission: frescos for the Pilar Cathedral, Saragossa.

1772 Birth of Vicente Lopez.

1773 Goya marries Josefa Bayeu, sister of Francisco and Ramón Bayeu.

1774 Goya invited by Mengs to paint cartoons for the Royal Tapestry Factory of Santa Barbara. First dated portrait: Don Pedro Alcántara de Zúñiga.

5

1775 **First tapestry cartoons.**
> 1775 Gainsborough's portrait of the Duchess of Devonshire. Birth of Turner.
>
> 1776 Mengs leaves Madrid, returns to Rome. Death of Lorenzo Tiepolo in Madrid. Birth of Constable.

1778 **Goya begins a series of etchings after canvases by Velazquez.**
> 1778 Death of Piranesi.
>
> 1779 Death of Mengs and Chardin.

1780 **After submitting his "Christ on the Cross" (Prado), Goya is unanimously elected a member of the Academy of San Fernando.**
> 1780 Birth of Ingres.

1781 **Death of Goya's father at Saragossa. Receives a royal commission for one of seven altar-pictures for the new Church of San Francisco el Grande, Madrid.**

1783 **Portrait of the Count of Floridablanca (Urquijo Bank, Madrid).**

1784 **Inauguration of the Church of San Francisco el Grande. Goya's "St Bernardin of Siena preaching in the Presence of King Alfonso V" is adjudged the best of the seven altar-pictures. Birth of his son Xavier, the only one of his children to survive.**

1785 **Goya appointed Assistant Director of Painting at the Academy of San Fernando. Portraits of the Duke and Duchess of Osuna (Frick Collection, New York, and Juan March Collection, Majorca). First portrait for the San Carlos Bank: Don José de Toro y Zambrano (Bank of Spain, Madrid).**
> 1785 David's "Oath of the Horatii."

1786 **Goya appointed official painter of the tapestry factory.**

1787 **"Pradera de San Isidro" (Prado). Seven decorative paintings for La Alameda de Osuna.**
> 1788 Death of Gainsborough and Quentin de La Tour.

1789 **With the accession of Charles IV to the Spanish throne, Goya is appointed Court Painter. First royal portraits (Academy of History, Madrid). "The Family of the Duke of Osuna" (Prado).**
> 1789 Death of Joseph Vernet.

1791 **Goya begins his last tapestry cartoons.**
> 1791 Birth of Géricault.

1792 **While visiting his friend Sebastián Martínez at Cadiz, Goya falls seriously ill.**
> 1792 Death of Sir Joshua Reynolds.

1793 Eleven paintings for the Academy of San Fernando in which Goya gives free rein to "fancy and invention."

1793 Invention of lithography by Alois Senefelder. Death of Francesco Guardi, Ramón Bayeu and José del Castillo.

1794 Now stone deaf, Goya can henceforth communicate with others only by writing or sign-language. Portrait of La Tirana (Juan March Collection, Madrid).

1794 Death of Ramón de la Cruz.

1795 With the death of Francisco Bayeu, Goya succeeds him as Director of Painting at the Academy of San Fernando. Portraits of Francisco Bayeu (Prado) and the Duchess of Alba (Collection of the Duke of Alba, Madrid).

1796 Birth of Corot.

1797 Goya stays with the Duchess of Alba (now a widow) on her Andalusian estate of Sanlúcar. Portrait of the Duchess of Alba (Hispanic Society, New York). Advertising circular announcing the publication of The Caprices (82 etchings).

1797 Jovellanos appointed minister of justice. Marriage of Godoy with the Countess of Chinchón, daughter of the Infante Don Luis de Borbón and sister of Cardinal de Bourbon.

1798 Frescos for the Church of San Antonio de la Florida, Madrid. Six "witching" pictures for the Duke of Osuna. Portrait of Ferdinand Guillemardet, French ambassador to Spain (Louvre).

1798 Birth of Delacroix.

1799 Publication of The Caprices. Portrait of Moratín (Academy of San Fernando, Madrid). Portrait of Queen Maria Luisa (Royal Palace, Madrid). Goya appointed First Court Painter.

1800 Portrait of the Countess of Chinchón (Collection of the Duchess of Sueca, Madrid). "The Family of Charles IV" (Prado). Jovellanos comes under a cloud at Court.

1801 Birth of Bonington.

1802 Death of the Duchess of Alba.

1802 Birth of Constantin Guys. Publication of the Divine Comedy with illustrations by Flaxman.

1803 Portraits of the Count and Countess of Fernán-Núñez (Fernán-Núñez Collection, Madrid).

1804 (?) "The Maja Nude" and "The Maja Clothed" (Prado). Portrait of the Marquis of San Adrián (Diputación Provincial, Pampeluna).

1804 Gros paints "The Pest-House of Jaffa."

1805 Marriage of Goya's son Xavier with Gumersinda Goicoechea. Portrait of Xavier known as "The Man in Grey" (Noailles Collection, Paris).

1806 Birth of his grandson Mariano. Six panels illustrating the capture of the bandit Maragato (Art Institute of Chicago).

1806 Death of Fragonard.

1807 Portrait of the actor Máiquez (Prado).

1808 Napoleon's troops having occupied Spain, a War of Independence breaks out; uprising in Madrid on May 2. Equestrian portrait of King Ferdinand VII. Jovellanos is called back to Madrid.

1808 Birth of Daumier. Death of Hubert Robert.

1810 Goya works on the etchings of The Disasters of War.

1811 "The Bullet-Makers" and "The Powder-Grinders" (Escorial).

1811 Death of Jovellanos.

1812 Death of Goya's wife. Most of the works in his studio now pass into the hands of his son Xavier. Portrait of Lord Wellington (Wellington Collection, London).

1814 Restoration of Ferdinand VII to the Spanish throne; persecution of the liberals. "The Charge of the Mamelukes on May Second" and "The Shootings of May Third" (Prado). Goya harrassed by the Inquisition for having painted the two Majas. Birth of Rosario Weiss.

1815 Self-portraits (Academy of San Fernando and Prado).

1816 Publication of The Tauromachia.

1817 Trip to Seville to paint "Sts Justa and Rufina" (Seville Cathedral).

1819 Goya buys the Quinta del Sordo; falls ill at the end of the year. "The Last Communion of St Joseph of Calasanz," and then "Christ in the Garden of Olives" (Escuelas Pias, Madrid). Portrait of the Architect Don Juan Antonio Cuervo (Cleveland Museum of Art). Goya does his first lithographs. Opening of the Prado Museum.

1819 Géricault exhibits "The Raft of the Méduse" at the Paris Salon. Birth of Courbet and Jongkind.

1820 Revolt in Spain; the reactionary government of Ferdinand VII is overthrown. Goya attends a meeting at the Academy to swear allegiance to the liberal Constitution. Portrait of Tiburcio Pérez (Metropolitan Museum, New York).

1820-1822 The Black Paintings in the Quinta del Sordo (now in the Prado).

1822 Delacroix's "Barque of Dante."

1823 French troops under the Duke of Angoulême invade Spain and restore Ferdinand VII to the throne. Goya makes over the Quinta del Sordo to his grandson Mariano. Portrait of Don Ramón Satue (Rijksmuseum, Amsterdam).

1824 A wave of repressive measures against Liberals and many arrests; Goya goes into hiding until the storm passes. On May 30 he receives permission to leave Spain for France. July-August: he stays in Paris. September: he settles at Bordeaux with Leocadia Weiss and her two children. Portraits of Don José Duaso y Latre (Rodríguez Otín Collection, Madrid) and Moratín (Bilbao Museum).

1824 At the Paris Salon in August Delacroix exhibits "The Massacres of Chios"; Ingres, "The Vow of Louis XIII"; Lawrence, "The Duke of Richelieu"; Constable and Bonington, landscapes. Birth of Eugenio Lucas. Death of Géricault.

1825 Set of lithographs known as The Bulls of Bordeaux. Paints miniatures on ivory.

1825 Death of David at Brussels.

1826 Brief visit to Madrid where Vicente Lopez paints his portrait (Prado). Portrait of Don Santiago Galos (Barnes Collection, Merion, Pa.).

1826 Death of Flaxman.

1827 Another visit to Madrid. Portrait of Mariano (Private Collection, Madrid). Portrait of Don Juan Bautista Muguiro (Prado). "The Milkmaid of Bordeaux" (Prado).

1827 Death of William Blake.

1828 Portrait of Don José Pío de Molina (Reinhart Collection, Winterthur). Goya dies on April 16.

1828 Death of Bonington.

GOYA, PAINTER OF MAN

Goya left an immense body of work behind him: some 500 oil paintings, about 280 etchings and lithographs, and nearly a thousand drawings. (Any attempt to stake out the limits of his art or to embrace its infinite variety within the terms of a single definition or set formula is doomed to failure. Any such attempt, however astute, in some way belittles it or denies Goya some part of the enormous influence he has had on all painting since his time. We may think we know him, yet there are gaps in our knowledge both of the man and the artist—a veil of mystery shrouding not only several crucial periods of his life but several of his most important works.) Add to this the halo of legend that clung to the figure of Goya even in his own lifetime, and it will be granted that he presents something of a problem case.

But, for all the gaps, our knowledge of his life is the most reliable key we have to his work. (The story of his life spans 82 years, from 1746 to 1828, and its successive phases exactly correspond to the one thing we must grasp if we are to understand his art: its evolution in time and the peculiar rhythm of that evolution. What strikes us most when we try to sum up Goya's art are its violent contrasts and staccato breaks of continuity. Visitors to the Prado can hardly believe their eyes when they pass from his *Holy Family* to *The Shootings of May Third*, and from the Black Paintings of the "Quinta del Sordo" to *The Milkmaid of Bordeaux*. A gallery of pictures by Velazquez or El Greco is as harmonious and coherent as a roomful of Goya's is disconcerting. One lifetime, however long, seems hardly long enough for such versatility as this. In vain do we apply our

◄ PORTRAIT OF DON MANUEL OSORIO DE ZÚÑIGA, 1788. (50 × 40″)
BY COURTESY OF THE METROPOLITAN MUSEUM OF ART, NEW YORK.

usual notions of environment and evolution as we cast about for an explanation; these the complex nature of Goya's art completely defies.

There were three sharp breaks in his career. So sharp in fact, so drastic, that we get the impression of an ever widening gulf between the world he lived in and the progress of his art. What seems to emerge is a rhythm conforming to the four great periods of his life. First, up to 1793, came the incredibly slow rise to maturity of a painter whose peculiar gifts and temperament forced him to spend thirty years trying to find himself. This was a busy period, characterized to begin with by false starts and repeated setbacks in his striving to gain recognition, then by worldly success and happy, effortless achievement, serenely reflected in the tapestry cartoons.

In 1793 Goya was struck down by a severe illness that, while it left him stone deaf, suddenly released the pent-up creative forces within him. Thereafter he stamped his genius on his age, which accepted its indelible imprint without ever quite grasping what it meant. His most eloquent message is written across the ceiling of the Church of San Antonio de la Florida in Madrid. Long unnoticed or almost so, owing to their distance from the floor below, these frescos have now been revealed, thanks to modern photography, as one of the supreme works of art in existence.

Then came the second break, as fateful for his country as for Goya himself this time: the Napoleonic invasion of Spain in 1808 and the grim period of bloodshed and disorder that ensued. Appalled by the atrocities and the human suffering he witnessed, Goya voiced his feelings in that tragic masterpiece, *The Shootings of May Third*.

Finally, in 1819, after a second spell of illness followed by an uprush of mysticism, he embarked on his weirdest, most powerful set of paintings, the so-called *pinturas negras* with which he covered the walls of the house to which he had retired outside Madrid, the "Quinta del Sordo" (Deaf Man's House), as his neighbors called it.

These, then, are the high points of his art: the tapestry cartoons (1775-1792); the frescos in San Antonio de la Florida (1798); *The Shootings of May Third* (1814); and the Black Paintings of the Quinta del Sordo, now in the Prado (about 1820-1821). Each of these key works is exactly paralleled by a set of etchings: those made after Velazquez (1778); *The Caprices* (1799); *The Disasters of War* (1810-1820); and the *Disparates* (or *Proverbs*) (1820-1824).

Out of these bewildering metamorphoses from the frivolous elegance of the 18th century to the most daring anticipations of Impressionism and Expressionism, can any constant be said to arise, any guiding idea organically linking all these works together? The answer is yes, there *is* a constant from which scarcely a single work by Goya deviates, a common denominator of all his work, and that common denominator is the human being. Man's joys and humiliations, his dreams and follies, his hopes and hallucinations, his vileness, his inhumanity, his saintliness—these are Goya's sole preoccupation, he paints, etches, draws nothing else. No landscapes, no accessories, nothing but the barest backdrop, a lowering sky or the gathering darkness of a vaulted chamber—below, in the dead center, is always Man. This constant concern for living men and women and the means he devised to express it make Goya one of the great revolutionaries of painting. The frescos in San Antonio de la Florida reveal the full scope of the revolution he effected; they speak the very language of modern art.

SELF-PORTRAIT, DETAIL OF THE PORTRAIT OF FLORIDABLANC
URQUIJO BANK, MADRID.

IN SEARCH OF HAPPINESS

Goya is unusual among the major Spanish masters in that he came from northern Spain. Whereas Velazquez, Murillo and Valdés Leal all came from Seville, Zurbaran from the province of Estremadura, and Ribalta and Ribera from the Kingdom of Valencia, Goya was born (on March 30, 1746) at Fuendetodos, a poverty-stricken hamlet thirty-five miles from Saragossa. Both his father, a master gilder of considerable repute at Saragossa, and his grandfather, a notary in that city, probably belonged to a Basque family named Goya that had recently settled in Aragon. His mother, Doña Gracia Lucientes, came of a family of Aragonese nobles established at Fuendetodos. Hence the birth in this outlying village of Francisco de Paula José de Goya y Lucientes.

Brought up in daily contact with artisans and artists, young Goya first attended school at Saragossa, the Escuela Pía run by Ignorantine monks; there he met Don Martín Zapater, who became one of his closest friends, and with whom he kept up a lifelong correspondence. This is practically all that is known of his childhood. At fourteen he was apprenticed to José Luzán, a local artist trained in the school of the Neapolitan painter Solimena. How much talent Goya showed at this early stage is a moot point. Probably he was not a precocious student, but his father certainly did all he could to encourage the boy, hoping to fit his second son for something better than the trade of a mere artisan.

Goya spent four years in Luzán's workshop, where he learnt to draw by copying prints. But here he could hardly have seen or done anything that rose above mediocrity. Not only was the spark lacking that was to kindle his latent gifts, but his training at the hands of Luzán may have stunted his development for a time. That, anyhow, is the impression we get of this youthful period. Too wide a gulf lay between the humdrum art of the 18th-century Aragonese school and the slumbering fires of young Goya's personality for him to have gleaned anything vital or inspiring from Luzán, or from Bayeu or Mengs for that matter, whom he worked under later. And once he had shaken off their yoke, the only trace they left on him was a deep-seated loathing of the futile, soulless type of art they stood for.

Countless romantic tales, replete with duels and abductions, have been spun round Goya's youth, but of none is there any documentary proof. As far as we can tell, Goya entered quite matter-of-factly on his career as an artist, determined to make the best of what, at the time, was a highly honorable vocation, open to talented young men and holding forth the prospect of academic palms and lucrative Court commissions, not to mention fame and adulation. Two contemporary examples were there to spur him on. First of all, the Madrilenian painter Antonio González Velázquez, who had studied in Rome with Giaquinto and who, at twenty-four, had just decorated one of the domes of the Pilar Cathedral at Saragossa, thus introducing into Aragon the superficial, academic brilliance which his master, at this very time, was demonstrating in the new Royal Palace in Madrid. An even more recent example was young Francisco Bayeu, also one of Luzán's pupils, who had just returned to Saragossa after a two years' finishing course in Antonio González Velázquez' studio at Madrid.

Bayeu's junior by twelve years, Goya had still to complete his apprenticeship. But the news Bayeu brought him from the Court in Madrid must have whetted his ambitions. Charles III had come to the throne in 1759. A keen patron of the arts, eager to refurbish the luster they had lost in Spain, he summoned to Madrid the two most celebrated painters in Italy, Raphael Mengs and Giovanni Battista Tiepolo. Given a free hand in carrying out the king's projects, Mengs gathered a team of young Spanish artists around him, amongst whom he distributed lucrative royal commissions, singling out Francisco Bayeu in 1763 and José del Castillo in 1764.

Goya must have been very eager to win his share of the spoils, for in 1763, though only seventeen at the time, he competed for a scholarship at the Academy of San Fernando in Madrid. But not a single vote was cast in his favor and he came away empty-handed. In 1766 he again competed at the Academy, with exactly the same result. Not even Francisco Bayeu—now an established academician and jury member—voted for him and the gold medal was awarded to Ramón Bayeu.

Goya was presumably on intimate terms with the Bayeus by now, and Francisco (whose sister he was to marry) had probably taken him in hand and was coaching him. Possibly he had come in personal contact with Mengs and the Tiepolos. He may even have seen the great ceiling frescos by Giovanni Battista in the new Royal Palace, and these were the one revelation Goya's own time and milieu could offer him; all the rest was sterility. The elder Tiepolo (who died at Madrid in 1770) alone might have brought home to Goya the lesson neither Luzán, Bayeu, Mengs nor any other contemporary could have taught him: that true painting is born of daring, genius, the taking of unheard-of liberties, not of stale academic formulas and literary associations.

In 1771 we find Goya in Italy. How and when he came to make the trip is a mystery. All we know for certain is that in 1772 the Royal Academy of Fine Arts at Parma awarded him second prize in the competitions of the previous year. Yet Italy had more to offer than academic awards, and it is tempting to suppose that there at last Goya's eyes were opened to the meaning of painting, above all of color, which the frigid academicism of Mengs had all but done away with. Whom did he meet in Italy? Certainly not David, as some have alleged, since the latter did not go to Rome until 1775, and Goya had been back in Spain since 1771. Did he have any personal contact with Piranesi, whose prints were then so popular throughout Europe? The most we can say is that Goya admired Piranesi and collected his etchings, whose influence on him was by no means negligible. As for the extravagant cloak-and-dagger tales usually associated with Goya's stay in Italy, the less said the better. There is no foundation in fact for any of them, and they are quite out of keeping with the hard-working, academic-minded young painter he seems to have been.

The trip to Italy must have raised his prestige immensely. Hitherto he had made no headway at all in Madrid, but no sooner had he returned to Saragossa than commissions began to pour in. He may have learnt a good deal about fresco painting in Italy, and this would have stood him in good stead as the fresco technique was still little known in Spain. In the murals he began in 1771 for the Cathedral of Nuestra Señora del Pilar in Saragossa and the nearby Carthusian convent of Aula Dei, Goya, though following meekly in the footsteps of Luca Giordano and G. B. Tiepolo, proved his ability to turn out well-composed, well-executed work—whose interest today, however, is purely historical. The really amazing thing is that such dull and lifeless work as this could have been produced by the same man who painted *The Shootings of May Third* and *The Last Communion of St Joseph of Calasanz*. But it was Goya's destiny to begin with the Pilar frescos and to end, half a century later, with the lurid visions of the Quinta del Sordo, the frescos in San Antonio de la Florida standing midway between the two.

Settling in Madrid in 1774, Goya began plying his trade with the same monotonous mediocrity displayed by all his contemporaries. He had yet to show the slightest spark of genius, the faintest glimmering of the masterpieces to come. Goya's real apprenticeship, in fact, was just beginning.

In 1773 he had married Josefa Bayeu, sister of Francisco Bayeu who was now Court Painter and the protégé of Mengs, whose word was law in matters of art. With such good connections at Court, Goya must have felt that his fortune would soon be made. Hitherto he had specialized in religious pictures, chiefly frescos, but now he was caught up in an activity entirely new to him: the painting of tapestry cartoons.

The Royal Manufactory of Santa Barbara was working overtime to fill the orders pouring in for decorations for the king's various residences: the new Royal Palace in Madrid, his country seat at Aranjuez, the palace of El Pardo, the Escorial and La Granja. Like all Spanish sovereigns before him, Charles III was a great tapestry lover. But he had had enough of French and Flemish models, with their eternal round of biblical, mythological and genre themes (the latter invariably copied after Teniers and Wouwerman). In 1773, a year before Goya was invited to contribute, strict orders were issued to the Royal Manufactory concerning the subject-matter of their productions. The old themes were to be dropped as out of keeping with Spanish life; what was wanted now were hunting scenes, which the king and his son, the Prince of Asturias, later to reign as Charles IV, found more to their personal taste. The important thing about this change-over was that, for the first time, figures appeared in Spanish dress. From here it was only a step to figures and scenes typical of everyday Spanish life.

Goya's first commission was for a set of hunting cartoons intended to decorate the princes' dining hall at the Escorial. This early work (1775) is so singularly uninspired that it had always been ascribed either to Bayeu or to Maella. Yet these cold, crudely handled scenes are really Goya's, as has now been conclusively established. In them he conformed with complete docility to the stilted conventions of the academic circles in which he moved, to the example of his brother-in-law, to the tastes of the day, to the technical requirements of the tapestry weavers. But then he began to show his true colors. Once he had familiarized himself with this branch of painting, he began improvising with startling originality and quickly forged ahead of all his competitors. From 1776 on, he painted actual scenes of contemporary life to the exclusion of nearly all else. And remarkable scenes they were, smiling, carefree, lightly handled pictures of everyday life in Madrid: *The Picnic on the Grass, The Ball on the Banks of the Manzanares, The Sunshade, The Fair of Madrid, The Crockery Vendor, The Card Players* and many more. All the high spirits and charm of a people light-hearted, pleasure-loving and handsome by nature shine through these tapestry cartoons, just as they do in the contemporary sketches and satires of Ramón de la Cruz. This was the heyday of the *majos* and *majas*, whose fanciful costumes and amusements were taken up and made fashionable by the Spanish aristocracy, and of masques and open-air dancing on the banks of the Manzanares, of popular operettas on typically Spanish themes, of *zarzuelas, tonadillas* and *sainetes* that were the delight of Madrid's theater-goers. It was now that bullfighting first became the Spanish national sport, thanks to the exploits of such popular idols as Martincho, Costillares, Pepe Hillo and Pedro Romero. Welling up from the people itself, an immense wave of enthusiasm for all things typically, traditionally Spanish swept through every stratum of Spanish society towards the end of the 18th century, and even the Court was affected.

Over a period of seventeen years, from 1775 to 1792, Goya painted nearly sixty tapestry cartoons directly inspired by the most picturesque and colorful side of Madrid life, by the fiestas and amusements in which commoners and aristocrats rubbed shoulders and forgot class distinctions. Executed at irregular intervals (1775-1780, 1786-1788, 1791-1792), this group of works

THE SUNSHADE, 1777. (41 × 59¾″) TAPESTRY CARTOON. PRADO, MADRID.

bulks large in Goya's development. For all their seeming
frivolity, they were the anvil on which he hammered out his
superb technique and virtuosity. These cartoons left him free
to approach the subject as he saw fit and to test out the resources
of his imagination. But given the nature of his subject-matter,
he was also bound to respect the realities of everyday life, and
so he learnt to jot down what he saw at a moment's notice, to
record a glance, a movement, an attitude that had caught his
eye—in a word, to paint the truth at a time when most artists
were painting what was false and artificial.

21

THE CROCKERY VENDOR, 1778-1779. ($101\frac{3}{4} \times 86\frac{1}{4}''$) TAPESTRY CARTOON.
PRADO, MADRID.

THE FAIR OF MADRID, 1778-1779. $(101\frac{1}{4} \times 85\frac{1}{2}'')$ TAPESTRY CARTOON.
PRADO, MADRID.

23

Until 1780 Goya gave his whole time to his tapestry cartoons, producing about forty of them. His stock had begun to rise and his position at Court became securer day by day. In 1776 Mengs left Spain for Rome, where he died in 1779. For a while the Bayeus, Maella, del Castillo and Paret held the field in Madrid, propagating a decadent, hopelessly sterile brand of painting. But Goya began to exult in his powers and to measure them against the tide of wearisome mediocrity that washed up around him. And in the island of solitude where his genius had stranded him he discovered a companion: Velazquez. Towards 1778, having undertaken to make a set of etchings after Velazquez (probably he was commissioned to do so by the Count of Floridablanca, new minister of state), Goya was given access to the royal collections and there for the first time saw *Las Meninas* (which he etched) and many other paintings by his great predecessor, as well as a magnificent collection of works by Titian, Tintoretto, Veronese, Raphael, Van Dyck, Rubens and Rembrandt, which today are the pride of the Prado. Once this revelation had come over him, he saw things in a fresh light and, at thirty-two, as his real career began, he must have looked back at his own past with a contemptuous eye.

For the time being Goya capitalized on his discovery of Velazquez as best he could in eighteen second-rate etchings, which proclaim his incapacity for copying a given model. The one original feature of the work was purely technical: the use of aquatint, then something of a novelty. Twenty years later he used it again, testing out every possible effect of chiaroscuro, in *The Caprices*. But the influence of Velazquez took immediate effect in some of the tapestry cartoons, particularly in the backgrounds of *The Washerwomen* and *The Tobacco Guard*.

THE CROCKERY VENDOR (DETAIL), 1778-1779. TAPESTRY CARTOON. ▶
PRADO, MADRID.

25

Goya had begun to attract attention at Court. Received in 1779 by the royal family, he jubilantly informed his friend Zapater of the event, writing with all the ingenuousness of a bedazzled provincial: "I kissed their hands; never before had I felt such happiness." Next year, in 1780, he submitted his *Christ on the Cross* to the Academy of San Fernando. A solemn, spiritless work, but it was enough to secure his election to the Academy without a single dissenting vote. Hardly had he won the honor he had coveted so long than he sought to break free of such ties, especially that which was binding him ever more tightly to his brother-in-law Francisco Bayeu. Goya keenly resented being regarded as Bayeu's protégé, and when a commission for some new frescos at Nuestra Señora del Pilar at Saragossa came their way, he made a fierce show of independence and quarreled with Bayeu. Refusing once for all, as he wrote, to be "a mere executant, an employee in the pay (of his brother-in-law)," Goya seized the opportunity of making a stand against Bayeu and everything his elder symbolized in the way of hidebound academicism and smugness.

But in the end he backed down and the two men worked together as before. A day of reckoning, however, was not far off. Thanks to the good offices of Goicoechea, an influential friend of his at Saragossa, Goya was invited to contribute one of seven altar-paintings commissioned by the king for the church of San Francisco el Grande in Madrid. Others taking part in the work were Francisco Bayeu, Mariano Salvador Maella, Antonio González Velázquez and José del Castillo.

Goya labored for three years at this soul-killing task, which he dared not refuse. Bitter thoughts of his rebuff at Saragossa must have steeled him to see it through, though it was the most distasteful and unequal piece of work he ever did. His letters betray the disgust he had come to feel for painting, at least for a certain kind of painting. Nursing his grievance, he was half inclined to throw everything up for a quiet life at Saragossa with his good friend Zapater. There were only two things he really cared for, so he said—hunting and chocolate. But, knowing his honor as an artist to be at stake, he plodded on and finally finished his *Miracle of St Bernardin of Siena preaching in the Presence of King Alfonso V*, patterned after a work by Michel-Ange Houasse. Despite flashes of life and color here and there, it was a hopelessly second-rate painting, and yet it was adjudged the best of them all when the seven paintings were handed in in 1784. In it, though he was doing violence to his own genius, he took up the academic arms of his opponents and beat them at their own game. Still this concession stood him in good stead, since in 1786 it secured him the appointment of King's Painter. Provided with this sinecure for the rest of his life, Goya, now forty, was free at last to paint as he liked.

His first official portrait (1783) had been of the Count of Floridablanca, chief minister of state. Such a man might have proved an invaluable patron, but Goya painted him with unforgivable clumsiness, stiffness, heavy-handedness. In all this mismanaged composition a single detail catches our eye today: the figure of Goya himself on the left, in profile, an assertive young man obviously conscious of his own importance.

Though Floridablanca did next to nothing for Goya, this was not the case with two academicians who befriended him and smoothed his way into Court circles. One was Ventura Rodríguez, a well-known architect in the reign of Charles III, who opened the doors of Madrid society to him; it was through Rodríguez that he met the Infante Don Luis, the king's brother, whose family portrait he made at Arenas de San Pedro in 1783. His other benefactor was Don Gaspar Melchor de Jovellanos, future minister to Charles IV and the highest type of 18th-century Spanish aristocrat. He was Goya's lifelong friend and patron. Through him the artist broke into the circle of the most enlightened Spaniards of his day: Count Campomanes, Ceán Bermúdez, François Cabarrus, among others. They opened his mind to the ferment of new ideas, to the political, economic, social and moral problems that had completely escaped his notice hitherto. But to Jovellanos, above all, he owed several of his most important official commissions, notably the frescos in San Antonio de la Florida.

As early as 1784 Jovellanos secured him a commission for four altar-paintings in the church of the Calatrava College, Salamanca. In 1785 came the set of six portraits for the Bank of San Carlos (now in the Bank of Spain, Madrid). That year he received commissions from two of Spain's most illustrious noble houses: the Dukes of Medinaceli and the Dukes of Osuna. For the latter he painted in all nearly twenty-five pictures, the largest private collection of his works after that of the king.

From 1785 to the end of the century Goya enjoyed the most brilliant period of his career. Despite the terrible illness of 1792-1793, the great turning-point of his life, and despite occasional lapses into the facile and insignificant, he came steadily into his own, developing a technique and style whose consummate ease and freedom were unrivaled. He worked hard, lived intensely and tried his hand at every possible genre: official portraits, portraits of friends, portraits of children, tapestry cartoons, decorative paintings, religious pictures, mural paintings, genre scenes, allegorical pictures, drawings and etchings—a blaze of genius lighting up the somber, threatening sky of the late 18th century. To this glorious creative period belong four masterpieces: the frescos in San Antonio de la Florida (1798), *The Caprices* (1799), *The Family of Charles IV* (1800), *The Portrait of the Countess of Chinchón* (1800).

THE FLOWER-GIRLS (DETAIL), 1786. TAPESTRY CARTOON. PRADO, MADRID. ▶

Goya 8

The years 1785-1792 were happiest of all for Goya. His rising fame, his popularity at Court and with the élite of Madrid, a carefree life in the lap of luxury, the joy of being a father for the first time in 1784—all this threw a glow of happiness over everything he produced. Witness the tapestry cartoons of 1786, with a place apart for *The Flower-Girls* (or *Spring*), and above all the lovely decorations painted for La Alameda de Osuna, his noble patrons' country home on the outskirts of Madrid. Free at last of every constraint, Goya painted seven delightful anecdotal compositions whose grace and freshness of color are unique in his output. *The Swing, The Accident* (in which the Duchess of Alba is thought to appear for the first time) and *The Greasy Pole* are the most perfect things of their kind in 18th-century painting: misty backgrounds barely covering the canvas, small-scale figures and gay patches of color in the Spanish costumes.

The *Pradera de San Isidro* (1787), a tapestry cartoon that never reached the weaver, is a further token of Goya's abounding joy in life at this stage of his career. An apotheosis of Madrid, of the peculiar light of the place and its colorful populace, this "Fiesta of San Isidro" is easily the finest example of *peinture claire* produced in the century preceding Impressionism.

The portraits, however, represent the most advanced stage of his evolution at the time. The Alameda decorations and the *Pradera de San Isidro* mark a climax in Goya's work (his fond farewell to the carefree pleasures of late 18th-century life), whereas, on the contrary, his portraits of the same period herald the great portraits of his maturity. After getting off to an awkward start in 1783 with his over-elaborated portrait of Floridablanca, Goya strode rapidly towards a style both simpler

◀︎   THE GREASY POLE, 1787. (66¼ × 35″)
COLLECTION OF THE DUKE OF MONTELLANO, MADRID.

and truer, in which the sitter stands out strongly against a uniform background with a minimum of accessories. His palette changed accordingly; he clamped down on his early passion for truculent splashes of color and skillfully reduced them to elegant schemes of silver grey that are never cold or dull. In 1785 he painted *The Duke and Duchess of Osuna*; then the set of six portraits in the Bank of Spain (finished in 1788); in 1786 an austere and humorless *Francisco Bayeu* (San Carlos Museum, Valencia) and *The Marchioness of Pontejos* (Mellon Collection, National Gallery of Art, Washington), most rococo of all his portraits; then, from 1788 on, the wonderful portraits of children, *Don Manuel Osorio de Zúñiga* (Metropolitan Museum, New York), *Don Luis María de Cistue* (Rockefeller Collection, New York), the two children in the Edouard de Rothschild Collection, Paris, and the four Osuna children in the Prado—all these show Goya at his most tender-hearted and on that score alone are quite exceptional in the whole of Spanish painting. He would have nothing to do with the complicated, minutely detailed type of portrait of which the English and Flemings were so fond, but focused the entire interest of the picture on these frail children, whom he portrayed alone save for an occasional pet or favorite toy. Unlike most of his contemporaries, he took no account of his sitter's pedigree, refrained from flattery and did not linger over insignificant details.

Shortly before his illness, he painted a portrait of his friend *Don Sebastián Martínez* (Metropolitan Museum, New York), with whom he stayed for a while at Cadiz in 1792. This work inaugurates the famous period of Goya's grey-and-silver color-schemes, that last refinement of "form" and the crowning technical feat of 18th-century painting.

THE SWING, 1787. ($66\frac{1}{4} \times 39\frac{3}{4}''$)   ▶
COLLECTION OF THE DUKE OF MONTELLANO, MADRID.

33

THE SWING (DETAIL), 1787.
COLLECTION OF THE DUKE OF MONTELLANO, MADRID.

THE SWING (DETAIL), 1787.
COLLECTION OF THE DUKE OF MONTELLANO, MADRID.

THE SWING (DETAIL), 1787.
COLLECTION OF THE DUKE OF MONTELLANO, MADRID.

Of the seven paintings made in 1787 to decorate La Alameda de Osuna, *The Swing, The Accident, The Coach attacked by Bandits* and *The Greasy Pole* now belong to the Duke of Montellano, Madrid, and *The Injured Mason* (or *The Building of the Castle*) and *The Procession* to Count Romanones, Madrid; *The Herd of Bulls* was formerly in the De Nemes Collection, Budapest. These themes are typical of those Goya was then using in the tapestry cartoons, and in fact *The Swing* and *The Injured Mason* were practically duplicated in two such cartoons now in the Prado—with this difference, that here there are fewer figures and the brushwork is noticeably freer.

When Charles IV came to the throne in 1789, Goya was appointed Court Painter. But thoroughly alarmed at events in France, the new king lost no time in purging his régime of every "progressive" element and Goya's friends bore the brunt of his reactionary zeal. With every liberal regarded as a potential revolutionary, Cabarrus, Jovellanos and Ceán Bermúdez were imprisoned or exiled.

Until now Goya had been more concerned with enjoying life to the full than with criticizing what went on around him, and if anything—aside from being a great painter—was more of a *majo* and a *parvenu* than a philosopher. Then all at once in 1790, in a letter to Zapater, he announced a momentous decision. "I've given up going to places where I might hear them (the *seguidillas*) because I have got it into my head now that it's my duty to live up to a certain standard and maintain the dignity that a man should always possess. With all that's been going on, let me assure you, I'm far from satisfied." Blurted out with the usual clumsiness of Goya's utterances, this was his gruff farewell to the delights of that colorful, easy-going, pleasure-seeking Spain so severely condemned by his friends. But at bottom it was more than that, for though only dimly aware of it, Goya had crossed the dividing line: behind him lay the tapestry cartoons, ahead of him *The Caprices*. Often the same figures appear in both, but he had come to see them in a different light and from a different angle. Life went on as before at the Spanish Court, but Goya watched it with a critical, disapproving eye. His illness goading him on, he was soon producing his first caricatures; with these the 19th century began.

SELF-PORTRAIT (DETAIL), CA. 1793.
COLLECTION OF THE COUNT OF VILLAGONZALO, MADRID.

THE PAINTER OF SOULS

THE course of Goya's life and that of his art were sharply deflected by two momentous events. The first, in 1793, was the tragic illness that left him deaf; the second, in 1808, was the French invasion of Spain. Yet, though these affected him deeply, we must not lose sight of the innate peculiarities both of his temperament and his art, in particular the compulsion he felt, again and again, to rejuvenate his art, to strike out into the unknown without pausing over past achievements, however brilliant. Never did Goya feel that he had "arrived." The itch for fresh fields to conquer is perhaps the real secret of his eternal youth and the key to so much that is puzzling in his work. Had he not been so constituted, neither illness nor war nor any other emotional shock could have made him paint as he did.

Goya had his first attack at Cadiz in 1792. Whatever his disease was (at any rate not syphilis, as has often been alleged), it caused him intense physical and mental suffering. He pictured himself a dying man, cut off—to make matters worse—from his family and above all from his son Xavier, to whom he was deeply attached. Then, when his life was out of danger, he was left for a time with the right side of his body paralysed, with dizzy spells, a buzzing noise in his head and partial blindness. Finally he got back on his feet again, only to find himself irremediably deaf. For the rest of his life he was obliged to communicate with others by writing or by a sign-language, but this was not the worst. By all accounts, Goya's deafness was accompanied by roaring noises and headaches. Thus after throwing off his illness, he was not plunged into the healing solitude of complete silence, but into a world of chaotic rumblings and buzzings that fretted his nerves to the breaking-point.

On his return to Madrid, he went back to work at once. And as he stood alone before his canvas, his imagination seems to have spirited him away towards new subjects, or rather towards a new vision of the world he could see but no longer hear. Painting eleven pictures now, one after the other, for the Academy of San Fernando, he sent them in with a covering letter to the director, Don Bernardo Iriarte; this is one of the most precious documents we have from Goya's own hand. "In order," he wrote, "to occupy an imagination mortified by the contemplation of my sufferings and to recover, partially anyhow, the expenses incurred by illness, I fell to painting a set of pictures in which I have succeeded in giving observation a place usually denied it in works made to order, in which little scope is left for fancy and invention." He describes these works as "popular in appeal" and adds that one, as yet unfinished, represents a madhouse. Unfortunately, there is no way of proving that the five panel paintings now in the Academy of San Fernando—*The Burial of the Sardine*, *The Procession of the Flagellants*, *The Village Bullfight*, *A Scene from the Inquisition* and *The Madhouse*—originally formed part of that group. Judged on technical and stylistic grounds, they would seem to date from the period 1808-1815. But technique and style are no argument when we remember the leaps into the future (or the past) that Goya was capable of. So that until proof to the contrary is brought forward we may take it that these five masterpieces date from the nineties, immediately after his illness, and accept them as the first fruit of his new art, imbued as they are with all its tragic vehemence. They point to a radical change in his palette, dominated now by neutral tints (greys, blacks and browns) with acid touches of almost pure red, yellow and blue. Nor is his brushwork quite the same; strokes are shorter, more agitated, fretfully sowing clots of pigment on their path. For the first time Goya was painting for himself alone, regardless of rules or anyone else's opinion. In a way there is a family likeness to the tapestry cartoons, but transposed

and screen men's crimes and perversities from the eyes of the world. Subject-matter and technique joined to form a new style, peculiar to Goya and alien to his period, whether in Spain or elsewhere—a style so dynamic and original that, leaping fifty years ahead, it linked up with the very style of modern painting.

With the eleven paintings for the Academy of San Fernando late in 1793, Goya made it plain that his art had lost nothing of its characteristic driving force. It is true that in his letters to Zapater he admitted there were times when he lost heart and despaired of ever enjoying life again, but there was no sign of

THE VILLAGE BULLFIGHT, 1793. (18 × 28½") ON WOOD.
ACADEMY OF SAN FERNANDO, MADRID.

faltering in his art. Several portraits made soon after his convalescence vouch for his unimpaired mastery. First, that of *General Don Antonio Ricardos* (Prado), one of his earliest character studies of a man; then, like a fond souvenir of the years 1786-1787, the vaporous figure of *Doña Tadea Arias de Enríquez* (Prado), whose stylish robe of white muslin shot with pink stands out against a vague garden setting. But the years 1794-1795 brought three of the finest offspring of his new palette of softly evanescent greys and whites: the portraits of *La Tirana* (Juan March Collection, Madrid), *Francisco Bayeu* (Prado) and the *Duchess of Alba* (Collection of the Duke of Alba, Madrid).

La Tirana—stage name of María del Rosario Fernández— was one of the most popular actresses of the Madrid theater. She first appears in an earlier portrait by Goya (at the Academy of San Fernando), painted at the peak of her career. Shown half-length in 1794, she is a different woman, stout and a little flaccid, already showing signs of illness. But the glory of the picture is her white muslin dress; we get a complete and dazzling display of Goya's virtuosity in the shimmering translucence and lightness of all these folds, frills and flounces, beneath which, nevertheless, we distinctly feel the volumes of the body. This impression is subtly emphasized by the plain background from which this ghost of the past emerges, certainly one of the most fascinating figures Goya ever painted.

Thoroughly Spanish, too, is the portrait of the *Countess of El Carpio* (Beistegui Bequest, Louvre), which presumably dates from the same period. No other picture by Goya better justifies his fame than this portrait of a proud, melancholy noblewoman. Every neighboring canvas in the Louvre cuts a paltry figure beside its easy freedom and bold characterization. David and

PORTRAIT OF THE ACTRESS LA TIRANA, 1794. (44 × 31 ")
JUAN MARCH COLLECTION, MADRID.

44

PORTRAIT OF THE PAINTER FRANCISCO BAYEU, 1795. (44 × 33″)
PRADO, MADRID.

Ingres are out of their depth; they simply cannot hold their own beside Goya, who almost casually solves the problems they toil over painfully, and who, as against their smooth technical skill, offers the careless spontaneity of his genius.⌉

In the portrait of *Francisco Bayeu* (Prado) Goya pays farewell homage, the very year of his death (1795), to his brother-in-law, a friend in need in the early days, whose smugness and patronizing self-importance, however, he could never stomach. Painted in an exquisite range of greys, the portrait of Bayeu has all the strait-laced severity appropriate to the character of the man. Again the finest part of the picture is Bayeu's dress, one of the best things in silver grey that Goya ever did.

⌈As for the *Duchess of Alba* (1795), this is much more than a famous portrait; here begins a new phase of Goya's life, the one that has done most to fire the imagination of romantic-minded biographers and to attach a legendary glamour to the figure of Goya. Probably we shall never know the true story of his relations with the Duchess of Alba.⌉ Every historical mention of their liaison touches on the facts with tantalizing discretion, with the result that we see these two remarkable people through a haze of sentimental associations. And today it is impossible to behold either this portrait in white or its counterpart in black at the Hispanic Society in New York without a tingle of emotion that has nothing to do with art.

In 1795 the Duchess of Alba was thirty-three, sixteen years younger than Goya. She had been married to the Duke of Alba for twenty years, during which time her beauty and excentric behavior had made her the most talked-of woman at the Spanish Court. Reckless and headstrong, she had vied for favor with the Queen, Maria Luisa of Parma, in the days when the latter was still Princess of Asturias, and she was now the friendly rival of the Duchess of Osuna at Court. These three women summed up all the charm and decadence of 18th-century Spain,

47

and of the three the Duchess of Alba was by all accounts the most beautiful, the most adulated. Making light of her aristocratic standing and her immense fortune, she affected the fashions and manners of the "majos" (the overdressed young sparks of Madrid, the "zoot-suiters" and "teddy-boys" of Goya's time) and she carried these so far, got into so many scrapes and so brazenly flitted from one love affair to another that even the most tolerant members of the aristocracy were scandalized. This had been going on for years, but not until 1795 did Goya paint her portrait and that of the Duke, whereas he had been patronized by the Osunas ever since 1785. Even assuming that we have the Duchess of Alba in the two Alameda paintings, *The Swing* and *The Accident*, still it is a curious fact that Goya made no other pictures for the Albas prior to the portraits of 1795. Perhaps the well-known rivalry between the Duchesses of Alba and Osuna is sufficient explanation. Generally regarded since 1785 as painter in ordinary to the Osuna family, Goya seems to have had little or no contact with the Albas before his illness. Only afterwards, as far as we can learn, did he get on intimate terms with them. Two small scenes (also painted in 1795) seem to prove as much: one of them shows the Duchess throwing a scare into her old duenna, La Beata; the other shows La Beata contending against two naughty children (one is the Negro girl Maria de la Luz) who, tugging at her skirts, are trying to pull her to the ground. Now lost, these two sketches were no doubt dashed off in the Albas' home in between sittings for the two large portraits of the Duke and Duchess. The little Negro girl reappears, at about the same time, in a drawing (Prado, no. 426) from the so-called Sanlúcar Notebooks. The most reasonable assumption, then, is

PORTRAIT OF THE DUCHESS OF ALBA, 1795. (76¼ × 51″) ►
COLLECTION OF THE DUKE OF ALBA, MADRID.

49

that Goya's intimacy with the Duchess of Alba dates from the last five or six years of the century, when she was still in the full flower of her beauty. He painted her then in her long white gown dappled with glowing reds: willful, impetuous, triumphant, her commanding figure crowned with the head of thick black hair of which she was so proud, her outstretched arm pointing to the dedication written on the ground beside her. Goya's portrayals of her constitute a whole cycle of paintings, drawings and etchings, and this persistent recurrence of a single person—unique in Goya's work, except of course for the royal portraits—proves how big a part she played in his life from 1795 until she died in 1802.

Soon after the brilliant portrait in white (that of the Duke shows him pensively bending over his harpsichord with a sheet of music by Haydn in his hands), Goya probably grew intimate with the Duchess of Alba, the Duke having died in 1796. He is known to have stayed with her during the period of mourning at her Andalusian estate of Sanlúcar de Barrameda, near Cadiz. There, almost certainly, he made the second large portrait in black (Hispanic Society, New York). Again the outstretched arm, but here, instead of pointing to a respectful dedication, it calls attention to a double ring engraved with the names Goya-Alba. Also dating from this happy period, the drawings of the Sanlúcar Notebooks go to confirm the intimacy between the Duchess and her painter.

After an illness that, at forty-six, had forced him to the brink of death, Goya (like Balzac, a few decades later, with Madame Hanska) apparently experienced that anguished, agonizing love peculiar to men of fifty; proof of this is the famous unpublished etching in *The Caprices* entitled *Sueño de la mentira y la inconstancia* (Dream of Falsehood and Fickleness). Yet, all things considered, it was only a passionate interlude in his life.

His vigorous spirit invariably overcame the passions and suffering of his mind and body and drew enrichment and fresh inspiration from them. Nothing could be farther from the truth than the traditional, romantic view of Goya's liaison with the Duchess—that "passion of a lifetime," that "impress of one woman on all his work." These sentimental fantasies are completely invalidated by two well-established facts. First, the letter to Martín Zapater in which, for the first and last time to our knowledge, Goya speaks of the Duchess in bantering terms that betray anything but a lover: "You would have done better to come and help me do the Alba woman, who came round to my studio to have her face painted." Secondly, and above all, the fact that in 1812, after his wife's death, when her estate was being shared out, Goya so readily parted with the large portrait of the Duchess, making it over to his son Xavier.

The truth is that his love-affair with the Duchess of Alba is significant—historically and psychologically speaking—only insofar as it ties up with the change of heart that came over him after his illness of 1792. The world that had once seemed so stable and enjoyable was falling to ruin. The "good old days," the "enlightened despotism" of Charles III, with its fiestas and merry-making, were over; his best friends had suffered disgrace or exile; the French Revolution and the downfall of the monarchy in France touched off a panic of reaction in Spain; Maria Luisa, the infamous queen of Charles IV, secured the removal of Floridablanca, chief minister of state, and replaced him with Godoy, her lover; Spain sank into economic lethargy and every liberal tendency was brutally repressed. All this—from which the Duchess of Alba distracted him only temporarily—affected Goya deeply. Hitherto he had merely sympathized with his friends' liberal ideas, but now these gathered force within him and he boiled with passionate indignation which he found no words to express. All the

technical skill he had acquired in the past seemed useless to him, and as he sought for new channels of expression he moved, at one swoop, from the simple brush-drawings of old to satirical caricature, going far beyond Hogarth and the late 18th-century English caricaturists and preparing the way for 19th-century French caricature, though no later master of the genre ever quite equaled him. ‍

Published in 1799, the eighty-two *Caprices* were for years the work by which Goya was known abroad, long before his paintings began to circulate. The French romantics right up to Baudelaire found in him an inexhaustible source of inspiration. They acclaimed him as the prototype of the modern romantic artist and the pioneer of the grotesque as an aesthetic value. Yet there is no denying that Goya conceived his *Caprices* as pure satire in the purest 18th-century tradition. What are they, after all, but so many caustic lampoons of women and their fickleness, of society and its imbecilities, of marriage, folly in all its forms, witchcraft and its hideous rites, monks and all the dark powers of intolerance and cruelty? But satire in the name of what? Plate 43, originally intended as the frontispiece, is a clear enough answer: in the name of Reason. What Goya had in mind was something of a tract for the times, and this is confirmed by the circular announcing its publication. The artist, we are told, "was convinced that the criticism of men's vices and shortcomings might also come within the province of painting"—an earnest profession of faith worthy of an 18th-century rationalist.

And yet, like Goya's 19th-century admirers, we cannot help feeling that *The Caprices* do not really belong to the so-called Age of Enlightenment, and that such pungent satire as this made a complete and drastic break with classical aesthetics. Suffice it

◄ PORTRAIT OF THE COUNTESS OF EL CARPIO, MARCHIONESS OF LA SOLANA, CA. 1792. ($72 \times 48\frac{3}{4}''$) BEISTEGUI BEQUEST, LOUVRE, PARIS.

to compare them with Tiepolo's *Scherzi di Fantasia* and *Capricci*, or with Hogarth's moralistic Progresses. On the one hand we have the anecdote, the satirical scene, sometimes amusing, sometimes serious, but always rational; whereas Goya's *Caprices* plunge us headlong into an underworld of passion, invective, nightmarish effects. For the first time etchings were called upon to express the mad and monstrous, as Bosch had expressed them in painting. While in one hand he held high the banner of Reason and Humanity, with the other, whether unwittingly or not, Goya opened wide the floodgates of the Irrational. Artistically speaking, his use of the broad planes peculiar to the aquatint proved to be not only the most original but the most modern solution possible to the problems of light and shade in etching. Goya's chiaroscuro, which regulated the entire layout and became his unmistakable signature, brings *The Caprices* directly into line with the tradition of Rembrandt. As Beethoven extended the range of emotional expression in music, so did Goya extend it in the plastic arts, at much the same time.

The preparatory drawings (nearly all on exhibit at the Prado) are surprisingly numerous and varied. Off and on from 1793 to 1798 he drew and etched these satires, but when they finally appeared, as he tells us himself, they met with scant success. "They are mostly sought after by foreigners," wrote Goya, little suspecting that the few copies bought in Madrid and carried abroad would soon make him a famous man in France and England, so famous and popular in fact as an engraver and satirist that Goya the painter—for he was first and foremost a great painter—long remained undiscovered and unknown.

That he painted relatively little between 1793 and 1797 was of course due to his illness and, above all, to his increasing devotion to drawing and etching. From now on, as we gather from his letter to the director of the Academy of San Fernando, Goya had had enough of painting to order. With the eleven pictures donated to the Academy in 1793, he discovered the joy and exultation of working entirely on his own. But to the end of his life he was torn between the duties of his official position and an invincible desire to work in complete freedom.

In the preparatory drawings for his *Caprices*, he found line to be an ideal means of expression for the new art he had in mind. To each subject he added a caption whose wit and raillery are typically Goyesque. Brief and to the point, the comments fit in admirably with these vignettes of real life and give precise meaning (usually ironical but always profoundly human) to each incident pictured; they are a salient feature of Goya's black-and-white work. *The Disasters of War*, *The Tauromachia*, the *Disparates* (or *Proverbs*), some twenty lithographs and nearly a thousand drawings—all were products of the fresh burst of creative activity that followed his illness. Except for *The Caprices* and *The Tauromachia*, however, none of this work was known to Goya's contemporaries.

As for the paintings produced from 1793 on, though we can readily distinguish those painted to order (portraits and religious pictures) from those inspired by his own fancy—his "caprices," as he called them—we can see at once that Goya's genius, far-ranging, irrepressible as ever, had grown much more complex. By now, of course, he was no longer bound to comply with the whims of his patrons or the set formulas of Mengs and Bayeu. Appointed director of painting at the Academy of San Fernando in 1795 and First Court Painter in 1799, he could take the liberty of painting as he pleased and adjusting official commissions to his own style. And all subjects, however hackneyed or tedious, took on new life in his hands. Nevertheless, these miracles of artistry tend to vary with Goya's mood of the moment and for this reason are sometimes unequal in the extreme; hence the difficulties encountered when any attempt is made to date and classify them in the absence of documentary evidence.

WITCHES' SABBATH, 1798. $(17 \times 11\frac{3}{4}")$
LAZARO MUSEUM, MADRID.

THE BEWITCHED (PRIEST POURING OIL ON THE DEVIL'S LAMP), 1798.
($16\frac{1}{2} \times 11\frac{3}{4}$") BY COURTESY OF THE TRUSTEES, NATIONAL GALLERY, LONDON.

The years from 1789 on proved time and again how "capricious" Goya's genius had grown. But before we go into these later works, a few words about his position at Court. Since the long series of official portraits of Charles IV and Queen Maria Luisa painted in 1789 and 1790, shortly after the coronation, then the last set of tapestry cartoons in 1791, Goya had filled no other commissions of any note. No doubt his illness largely accounts for this, yet the interlude of seven years seems strangely long. A likely explanation is that with Cabarrus and Jovellanos out of favor and banished from Madrid, Goya too was under a cloud. This is all the more probable in view of the abrupt change in his fortunes once Jovellanos was reinstated and reappointed minister in 1797. During the next four years (till 1801, when Jovellanos was again exiled and imprisoned at Majorca) Goya received his most important royal commissions: the frescos in San Antonio de la Florida, several portraits of the king and queen, the large portrait of the family of Charles IV and—semi-official commissions—the portraits of Godoy, now created Duke of El Alcudia and Prince of the Peace, and his young wife, the Countess of Chinchón.

Thus the years 1798-1801 show us Goya at the peak of his official career, but at the same time, after twenty-five years in the king's service, they led up to his final break with the Court, for reasons not yet elucidated. This being so, the works of these years are of special interest as showing us how Goya succeeded in reconciling his highly developed personal style with the derelict conventions of official art.

Of all the work he carried out for the kings of Spain, none is grander and more impressive than the frescos he painted in the little church of San Antonio de la Florida. This modest hermitage in neo-classical style had then just been built by the architect Villanueva on the outskirts of Madrid, in a working-

close at hand—has all the vividness and instancy of pure expression and, though over 150 years old, it could hardly speak out more forcibly, in more modern terms, if it had been painted yesterday. Here an angel brings to mind a watercolor by Bonnard, there a woman in a white veil might be a Delacroix, or a swarthy face with rough-hewn features a Daumier—so it goes from wall to wall. Yet, as any visitor to the church can experience for himself, all these prophetic glimpses of the future are soon forgotten amidst these wonderful paintings and only the name "Goya," that name alone, lingers in the memory.

Also from 1798 dates a large altar picture painted for the sacristy of Toledo Cathedral: *The Betrayal of Christ*. Despite a clever play of light and shadow that brings out the figure of Christ amid the sinister forms of his enemies, it is impossible not to wonder if this canvas is really by the same man who had just painted the Florida frescos. The whole handling of the work betrays a laxity, an utter want of conviction that, all of a sudden, carries us back to so indifferent a performance as the San Francisco el Grande picture of 1784. The flame that had burned so bright at San Antonio de la Florida has gone out completely. But it was soon to blaze up again.

With the faintly histrionic portrait of the French ambassador to Spain *Ferdinand Guillemardet* (Louvre) and his admirable *General Urrutia* (Prado), Goya brought to a close one of the most prolific years of his career. Early in 1799 the Duke of Osuna made a large purchase of pictures: the famous *Pradera de San Isidro*, *The Four Seasons* (dainty, small-size variants of the 1786 tapestry cartoons) and two scenes of country life, one of them no doubt the *Hermitage of San Isidro on the Day of the Fiesta* (Prado) whose luminous gaiety comes very close to that of the *Pradera*. In July—apparently at a single sitting—he painted the magnificent portrait of his friend the poet and dramatist *Leandro Fernández de Moratín* (Academy of San Fernando). Loyal to all his friends, whatever their political color, Goya made a whole gallery of portraits of writers, statesmen, painters and other intimates: in 1797 the poet *Juan Meléndez Valdés*, the academician *Don Bernardo de Iriarte*, and *Don Martín Zapater*; in 1798, *Don Gaspar Melchor de Jovellanos* and perhaps the painter *Don Asensio Julia*.

Still in favor at Court, Goya painted several large portraits of the king and queen, including the two equestrian portraits in the Prado. In her letters the queen kept her paramour Godoy informed as to the progress of the work and provided for copies (probably by Agustín Esteve, who worked in close collaboration with Goya in the last years of the century) to be made especially for him. The best of the queen's portraits (Royal Palace, Madrid) shows her dressed in black as a *maja*, wearing a mantilla set off with pink ribbons. Flattering and ruthless at the same time, it lifts the appalling, vice-ridden ugliness of Queen Maria Luisa on to a plane of pure Beauty; here, as in *The Caprices* and certain figures at San Antonio de la Florida, Goya founds a new aesthetic on the hideous and the horrible. Painted a little earlier, another portrait in the Royal Palace shows the queen in a sumptuous grey and white robe cut very low over her matronly bosom, splendidly triumphant in her sheer ugliness; in this prelude to the great portrait of the royal family Goya used a thick, vigorous impasto almost impressionistic in the treatment of details of the robe and jewels. Everywhere we feel the feverish haste of a master hand that never stops to correct or touch up, whose excited brushing juxtaposes tones outright instead of blending them into one another.

PAGE 66: PORTRAIT OF CARDINAL DE BOURBON, CA. 1798-1800. (78½ × 41½")
MUSEU DE ARTE, SÃO PAULO, BRAZIL.

PAGE 67: PORTRAIT OF THE COUNTESS OF CHINCHÓN, 1800. (82½ × 51")
COLLECTION OF THE DUCHESS OF SUECA, MADRID.

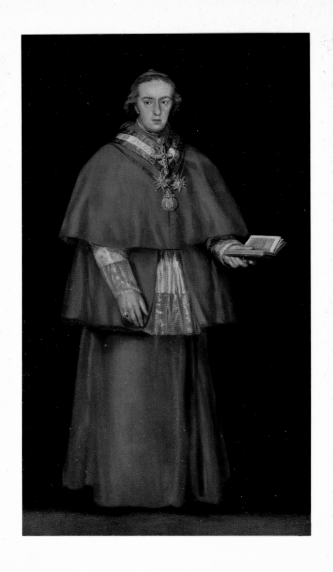

67

THE FAMILY OF CHARLES IV, 1800. (110 × 132″) PRADO, MADRID.

By 1800 Goya had reached the peak of his official career, having been appointed First Court Painter in October 1799. He made preliminary studies for his portrait of the Royal Family at the Palace of Aranjuez in June 1800; the finished picture was probably ready by the end of the summer. Group portraits are something of a rarity in Goya's work. Prior to this one, only two others are known: *The Family of the Infante Don Luis* (1783) and *The Duke and Duchess of Osuna and their Children* (1789). *The Family of Charles IV* was the last royal commission Goya received.

Goya's superb mastery of the portrait—always painted with a full brush and a brilliant, gemlike palette—reached its peak in 1800 with the *Family of Charles IV* (Prado) and the *Countess of Chinchón* (Collection of the Duchess of Sueca, Madrid).

Daughter of the Infante Don Luis, the Countess of Chinchón was then twenty-one. In Goya's eyes she must have been a charming reminder of the happiest days of his youth, his first taste of success at Arenas de San Pedro seventeen years before and the tiny girl of four he had painted there in the large portrait of the Infante's family. Married since 1797 to Godoy, she was still hardly more than a child. She bore in silent resignation the affronts and infidelities of her husband, who at official dinners maliciously relegated her to a place beside his mistress Pepita Tudó. An incurable busybody, the queen took a dictatorial hand in all the intrigues that kept this "triangle" from lapsing into respectability. By the force of circumstances, the unhappy Countess was an innocent party to the corruption and vice around her. But decent people of all classes, Jovellanos first of all, made no secret of their sympathy for the young noblewoman whose humiliations had come to symbolize the ignominy of the Court. All this—plus the pregnancy she shyly tries to conceal—Goya expressed magnificently with the same brushes that were soon to unmask the royal family. Pitiless towards the depraved old queen and those who fawned on her, he was all tenderness, all compassion for the poor young Countess, and few of his portraits possess such unity of feeling.

Probably dating from 1800, too, is the portrait of *Cardinal de Bourbon*, brother of the Countess of Chinchón. The finest version of this work is now in the Museum of São Paulo in Brazil. Though obviously turned out at high speed—the decorations worn by the Cardinal are only hastily sketched in—it is a portrait of great beauty and brilliance, in spite of the melancholy cast of the face.

With such works as these to his credit by June 1800, Goya felt ready to cope with the test of a portrait painter's powers: the large family portrait, and in this case—to complicate matters—the royal family. Two precedents, which he had had plenty of time to study and analyse, proved invaluable as working models, one showing him the target to aim at, the other the pitfalls to avoid. The first was *Las Meninas*, by Velazquez, which he had etched in 1778; the other was the pompous *Family of Philip V*, made in 1743 by Louis-Michel Van Loo.

To begin with, Goya painted a dozen or so preliminary studies of the leading members of the royal family—sketches from the life, as acutely penetrating as any of his mature portraits, which served to acquaint him intimately with his models' features. Apart from these, however, no group study, either drawn or painted, has come down to us, and we may take it for granted that, as usual, Goya painted the finished picture at one go. The chief problem, that of settling on the most natural, most plausible presentation of the figures, was more or less solved for him by the example of Velazquez. As in *Las Meninas*, the royal family is apparently paying a visit to the artist's studio, and we glimpse the artist himself on the left, facing us, but half hidden in shadow as he works at his canvas, of which we see only the back. At this point the resemblance with Velazquez stops. In *Las Meninas* the king and queen, unseen, pose in front of the artist and their image is dimly reflected in a mirror at the back of the room; here we are led to wonder if someone else is not striking the pose, confronting the royal family and Goya. Xavier de Salas has boldly suggested that this unseen figure out in front, whose presence we sense and at whom the queen seems to be gazing, must be Godoy, the only person important

THE FAMILY OF CHARLES IV, 1800. DETAIL: THE INFANTE DON FRANCISCO ▶
DE PAULA ANTONIO. PRADO, MADRID.

71

enough to justify so imposing an array of royalty. But surely this is a misinterpretation of the scene. Goya himself is there because the portrait depends on him and though he is proud to be seen carrying out his duties as First Court Painter, modesty bids him remain in the background. As for the royal group he seems to be sizing up, he has disposed it in peculiar fashion to suit his own ends. Whereas in *Las Meninas* we are struck by the atmospheric perspective of the palace interior, further extended to the rear by the door opening out on a world of light, what strikes us in *The Family of Charles IV* is the subtly conveyed effect of imminent suffocation; the room in which these people stand is like a cell without an exit. They seem to be assembled, not in a room of the Royal Palace, but on a stage facing the public, while in the shadow of the wings the painter, with a grim smile, points and says: "Look at them and judge for yourself!" Staging this royal comedy with a consummate sense of the theater, Goya weaves the magic spell of his brush over these beribboned, overdressed actors. Drunk with light, he spatters jewels and garments with pigment rich in gold, vivid reds and deep blues; absurd figures, anything but majestic, frozen by vanity and pretence, he melts them into a vibrant mass of dazzling light and mingled shadows, out of which the set faces stare, guilelessly proclaiming the hollow smugness of their royal souls.

This devastating portrait was the last commission Goya executed for the royal residences, and though until his death twenty-eight years later he continued to draw the salary attaching to his official position, in reality he did nothing to earn it. The real reasons for his semi-official retirement are not known. It has been alleged that a dispute arose between the king and his painter over the princess with her face turned away on the left in the portrait of the royal family, whose features Goya (so it is said) flatly refused to paint. Be this as it may, a more important point to bear in mind is that in 1801 Jovellanos, an old friend to whom Goya was loyally attached, was thrown into prison and there remained until the revolution of 1808. Furthermore, the Duchess of Alba had died in 1802 in rather mysterious circumstances—though it cannot be said for certain whether Goya keenly felt her loss or not. What affected his position more seriously was the arrival at Court of Vicente Lopez, whom Charles IV appointed Court Painter in 1802 and whose die-hard academicism may well have outweighed Goya's genius in the king's estimation. Possibly *The Caprices* finally turned the king against Goya. In 1803 at any rate—perhaps to ease the strain in their relations—Goya presented him with the copper plates of the etchings and 240 unsold copies of the printed book. In return the king granted a pension to Goya's son Xavier, now a youth of nineteen.

THE MAJA CLOTHED, CA. 1804. ($37\frac{1}{4} \times 74\frac{3}{4}''$) PRADO, MADRID.

73

Nevertheless, after a brilliant period in the limelight from 1798 to 1800, Goya begins to slip away from us and the facts of his life grow meager and shadowy. With his best friends, Jovellanos and Ceán Bermúdez, imprisoned or in exile and others, like the Duchess of Alba, having passed away, he seems to have taken refuge in solitude, painting chiefly portraits commissioned by private persons (most of these date from 1805) and devoting himself more and more to drawing and sketching; this, in fact, was to become his consuming passion and the great reservoir of forms and ideas for his later work.

From 1801 dates his last official portrait: that of Godoy (Academy of San Fernando), dressed up as a conquering general after the brief and successful war against Portugal in that year. This grandiose tribute to the glory of the royal favorite brought Goya to the close of the most brilliant period of his career.

But before we move on from this farewell to Godoy—who, whatever the frivolity with which he governed Spain, was one of Goya's most appreciative patrons—mention must be made of two well-known canvases that all visitors to the Prado make a special point of seeing, always at the expense of much finer works far more deserving of interest but mistakenly regarded as being less "Goyesque." I refer to the two *Majas*, whose fame—or notoriety—is largely due to the traditional belief that the Duchess of Alba posed for them. The most authoritative Spanish critics have conclusively shown that this plump, rather thickset young woman is anyone but the Duchess of Alba. Yet the aura of scandal persists and accounts for the popular fallacy that these are Goya's masterpieces. Painted some time before January 1st, 1808 (when we find them listed in an inventory of Godoy's assets), the two *Majas* betray a distinct slackness of touch that has nothing in common with the tenderness infusing the portrait of the Countess of Chinchón and that of Doña Isabel Cobos de Pórcel (National Gallery, London).

PORTRAIT OF THE COUNT OF FERNÁN-NÚÑEZ (DETAIL), 1803.
COLLECTION OF THE DUCHESS OF FERNÁN-NÚÑEZ, MADRID.

PORTRAIT OF THE ACTOR DON ISIDORO MÁIQUEZ (DETAIL), 1807.
PRADO, MADRID.

In being deliberately sensual (he was probably catering to the appetites of Godoy), Goya could not help lapsing into a certain mawkishness. No doubt the *Maja Nude* is a landmark in the rather prudish annals of Spanish painting, but the truth is, paradoxically enough, that the *Maja Clothed* goes one better as far as sensuality and sheer opulence of effect are concerned. We might add that Manet's *Olympia*, so often compared to the *Maja Nude* and certainly akin to it in conception, is, aesthetically speaking, worlds away from the boudoir realism of doubtful taste that Goya affected in the two *Majas*.

From about the same period we have two of Goya's finest full-length portraits of men. The first, dating from 1803, is that of the *Count of Fernán-Núñez* (Collection of the Duchess of Fernán-Núñez, Madrid); the second, dating from 1804, that of the *Marquis of San Adrián* (Diputación Provincial, Pampeluna). In both Goya seems intent above all on bringing out the modeling of the body and the elegance of the posture. Count Fernán-Núñez, in particular, draped in his dark cape against a distant landscape in twilight and a sky sagging with storm-clouds, has all the noble dignity of a great Spanish *hidalgo*.

The year 1805 was a prolific and a happy one for Goya. He now possessed a comfortable fortune, and in 1803 had even purchased a second house. This he made over to his son Xavier, who in July 1805 had married into the Goicoechea family and the following year presented his father, now sixty, with the grandson, Mariano, on whom he doted in his old age and whom he lovingly painted several times. To commemorate these happy events Goya made the large portrait of Xavier known as *The Man in Grey* (Noailles Collection, Paris). This is the only portrait positively known to represent Xavier, and in it he appears exactly as he seems to have been throughout his life: a man of inordinate vanity who lived for money and the luxuries it could buy. Of all Goya's male portraits, this one

MARAGATO THREATENS FRAY PEDRO DE ZALDIVIA, 1806. (11½ × 15¼")
ON WOOD. OWNED BY THE ART INSTITUTE OF CHICAGO
(MR AND MRS MARTIN A. RYERSON COLLECTION).

and those of the Marquis of San Adrián and the Count of
Fernán-Núñez are most evocative of English portrait painting, in their conscious striving to show an elegant full-length
figure to best advantage.

In 1806 Goya painted a set of six small panels illustrating a
current event that was then the talk of Spain: the capture of

FRAY PEDRO DE ZALDIVIA BINDS MARAGATO, 1806. ($11\frac{1}{2} \times 15\frac{1}{4}''$)
ON WOOD. OWNED BY THE ART INSTITUTE OF CHICAGO
(MR AND MRS MARTIN A. RYERSON COLLECTION).

Maragato, a notorious highwayman, by the monk Pedro de Zaldivia. Dashed off in rapid succession with Goya's usual brio, these panels set forth the incident in the spirited narrative style of present-day comic strips. They are, moreover, a perfect example of Goya's imaginative realism, one of the distinctive traits of his art.

Many of Goya's portraits date from 1805-1806: *Don José de Vargas y Ponce* (Royal Academy of History, Madrid), the *Marquis of Santa Cruz* (Felix Valdés Collection, Bilbao), *Don Felix de Azara*, *Leonor Valdés de Barruso* and *María Vicenta Barruso y Valdés* (formerly Orossen Collection, Paris), *Doña Isabel Cobos de Pórcel* (National Gallery, London) and her husband *Don Antonio Pórcel* (Jockey Club, Buenos Aires), *Don Tadeo Bravo del Rivero* and the *Marquis of Espeja* (Collection of the Duke of Valencia). Undated but no doubt contemporary are the beautiful portraits of Don Bartolomé Sureda and his wife (Frelinghuysen Collection, Morristown, N.J.).

The fruit of Goya's serene maturity, all these portraits might have led people to believe that the vein of inspiration from which had sprung *The Caprices* and so many genre scenes had dried up altogether. Such was by no means the case and it is a point worth stressing that Goya's deepest vision of men and things is to be found precisely in the many drawings of this period. Lightly drawn for the most part in India ink with the tip of the brush, all have a sureness and simplicity of design worthy of Rembrandt. The note they strike is not so much that of caricature as of realism, now grotesque, now compassionate, driven home with a crisp caption even more effectively —if that is possible—than in *The Caprices*.

In 1807, on the eve of the tragic events about to befall Spain, he painted one of his most moving male portraits, that of the actor *Don Isidoro Máiquez* (Prado). The man must have been a close friend of Goya, to judge from the warm sympathy with which he conveyed the sensitivity and intelligence of this fine face, imbued though it is with a vague romanticism in the manner of Chateaubriand, whose novel *René* had just appeared at Madrid in a Spanish translation in 1806.

THE WATER-CARRIER, CA. 1810. (26¾ × 19¾″) BUDAPEST MUSEUM. ▶

82

Fifteen years had passed since the sudden illness that had so deeply affected both the manner of his life and the style of his art. By now, at sixty-two, Goya had accomplished more than enough to alter the entire course of European painting. And when we remember what painting was like in the first decade of the 19th century, in Spain and elsewhere, we can hardly believe our eyes as we take in the superb freedom, boldness and modernity of such a work as the frescos in San Antonio de la Florida, whose significance has not yet been given its due. *The Caprices*, brought out in 1799, struck the French romantics thirty years later as incredibly bold and "advanced." As for his technique both as a painter and engraver, diverging radically from the lines of 18th-century art, it contained in embryo every subsequent discovery made by Impressionism and Expressionism and completely shattered the academic chains that were strangling art. Yet up to this time Goya's revolution had had its limits, and in spite of the monsters, witches and nightmarish visions of *The Caprices*, we cannot really speak of any tragic sense of life in his work prior to 1808. Caricature and satire, shrewd insight into men and things, an occasional revelation of human suffering, yes—but as yet neither anguish nor hallucination.

Goya still had twenty years to live, twenty grueling years that were to lead him to ventures even bolder than before. With a fresh burst of energy, he seemed to enter on a second life, no less fecund than the life that had just ended so serenely, but more intense and stormy. Deeply human and as always thoroughly Spanish, for all his advanced age and physical infirmities Goya now shared to the full the disasters that overtook his country, and in the fires of a cruel war forged a new art for the new times to come.

◄ THE KNIFE-GRINDER, CA. 1810. ($26\frac{3}{4} \times 19\frac{3}{4}$") BUDAPEST MUSEUM.

SELF-PORTRAIT AT THE AGE OF 69, 1815. (18 × 15¾″)
ACADEMY OF SAN FERNANDO, MADRID.

THE TRAGIC SENSE OF LIFE

THE events that suddenly turned the eyes of Europe on Spain can hardly be gone into here at any length, but were briefly these. By 1808 the reign of Charles IV had become one long catalogue of political and social blunders. This, coupled with the corruption of his government and the power politics and ambitious schemings of Napoleon, consummated Spain's downfall and plunged the country into war and revolution. When in March 1808 Madrid was occupied by a French army under Murat, the Spanish monarchy ignobly collapsed. The old king, pensioned off by the French government, retired to Rome. His son Ferdinand VII was brushed aside for the time being and Napoleon placed his brother Joseph on the Spanish throne.

Joseph Bonaparte was a well-intentioned man who did his best to preserve order and peace. But his "subjects" bitterly resented his presence, Napoleon continually meddled in his policies, and revolt soon became only a question of time. On May 2, 1808, an uprising in Madrid was savagely put down by French troops, but thereafter a guerilla war of independence made rapid headway in the provinces. For the next six years war, rapine and famine rained disaster down on a country already desperately poor, but inflexibly proud and courageous. When Ferdinand VII regained his throne in 1814, Spain's political convulsions began afresh. Not a single Spaniard but in these years had to opt for one side or the other and steer a course of his own through a period of squalid confusion due to war, invasion and the restoration of absolute monarchy.

What stand did Goya take in these troubled times? For some he symbolizes the heroic resistance of the Spanish people to the French invaders, whom he arraigned so fiercely in *The Disasters of War* and the two famous canvases at the Prado, *The Charge of the Mamelukes on May Second* and *The Shootings of May Third*.

For others, on the contrary, he was the typical *afrancesado* in view of his well-known liberal sympathies and the favors and commissions he accepted from the French during the occupation. But the truth is not so simple, for in Goya, as in many Spanish intellectuals of that day, there were two men, usually at odds with each other. First the Progressive, the Liberal (exemplified by Jovellanos), who insisted on sweeping political and social reforms and pinned his hopes for these on France, cradle of freedom and new ideas. But then, in the face of foreign invasion and the ruthless strangling of his country's vital forces, there was also the proud and resentful patriot who took up arms and fought back. In Goya's case a third factor came into play and went far towards reconciling these opposing tendencies. This, in a word, was his innate prudence. Ever since his youth Goya, for all his temperamental violence and obstinacy, had shown that he could also be cautious and diplomatic. A man of the people, he had always been impressed by the great of the world and, whatever his disgust with the intrigues and corruption of the Court, never did he permit himself a direct thrust at either the king, the queen or Godoy. Even *The Caprices*, whatever their implications, never exceed the bounds of discretion and prudence, and the keys to their "real" meaning are as arbitrary as those professing to explain *Les Caractères* of La Bruyère.

Throughout the political storms that broke over Spain after 1808 Goya successfully held a middle course, retaining his post of First Court Painter under Joseph Bonaparte as he did under Ferdinand VII. He was even decorated by the "Intruder King" and made portraits not only of the Spanish officials who collaborated with the French but of the French generals who scourged Spain. And once they had been driven out, this did not prevent him from painting General Palafox, the hero of Saragossa, and the Duke of Wellington, the liberator of Madrid, nor from etching *The Disasters of War* and even applying for official permission "to commemorate with my brush the exploits, the most remarkable and heroic episodes of our glorious insurrection against the tyrant of Europe." Behind the façade he put up to safeguard the position and benefits it had cost him thirty years to achieve, we have no difficulty in discerning the real Goya; *The Disasters of War* and countless drawings can leave no doubt in anyone's mind. He hated Napoleon's soldiery for the havoc it wrought in Spain, but he also felt an immense contempt for the idle, bigoted, parasitic monks and priests who paralysed his country and drained its life-blood. A Frenchman on the Spanish throne was an unbearable affront to the Spaniard in him, but the despotic, petty-minded absolutism of Ferdinand VII was no less galling. What Goya, like so many Spaniards, yearned for was a liberal government of honest, responsible patriots capable of carrying out much-needed reforms, while he looked to France not for an invasion by arms but for an invigorating flow of new ideas. This in effect was what the Cortes of Cadiz (a meeting of the chief reforming parties held at Cadiz in 1810) and the Constitution of 1812 promised Spain. But the return of Ferdinand VII smothered every hope and spelt wanton misrule. Goya voiced his feelings in the last etching of *The Disasters of War*, where we see Truth dying miserably under the complacent gaze of the powers-that-be.

During the war he painted every portrait asked of him without inquiring into the politics of the sitter. So there is no apparent gap in his work before and after the war, and no change of any note, at least in the field of the portrait. When Ferdinand VII first came to the throne in 1808, the Academy at once commissioned Goya to make an official portrait of him. As far as we can tell, this is the only portrait for which his royal model sat in person. From Goya himself, who apologizes for the fact, we learn that the young king deigned to pose only twice, for a bare three-quarters of an hour each time. This equestrian portrait (Academy of San Fernando) is the most faithful and least ridiculous of all Goya's portraits of Ferdinand VII. But, ironically enough, by the time he notified the Academy that it was ready, the king had been sent into exile.

Meanwhile the historic events of May 2, 1808, had taken place. Fierce street-fighting between the insurgents of Madrid and Murat's troops ended in the victory of the latter, who promptly retaliated by mass executions. On May 3rd French firing-squads were particularly active and no one was safe in the streets. Goya's two famous pictures of these events, though not painted until 1814, must have been inspired by scenes he actually witnessed, so intense is the emotion they convey. But we find ourselves again in the realm of legend and pure fantasy when, as they are wont to do, Goya's biographers picture him at his windows on the Puerta del Sol watching the dramatic charge of the Mamelukes and the Imperial Guard on May 2nd. Or, again from his windows, but this time in the Quinta del Sordo beyond the Manzanares, watching the firing-squads mow down their victims in the dead of night. Or, as some accounts would have it, roaming the dark streets with a faithful servant and sketching the corpses by lamplight before they had even grown cold.

This lurid romanticizing has been thoroughly discredited by the research-work of such authorities as Mr Sánchez Cantón and the Marquis of Saltillo. We now know that in 1808 Goya and his wife were living in the Calle Valverde (behind the present-day Telephone Building) at some distance from the Puerta del Sol. As for the Quinta del Sordo, he did not buy it till 1819. From his own windows, then, Goya could not possibly have been an eye-witness of these events. However, like so many who were anxious to see what was going on, he may have gone down into the streets on that memorable day. Even many years later at Bordeaux, though he had turned eighty, he still made a habit of roaming the streets and observing people and things. Knowing Goya, we can practically take it for granted that he went out to see the riots for himself. And even assuming he was not an actual eye-witness, he must have heard many firsthand accounts from those who were. Thus he may safely be said to have lived through the events of those two historic days, and on his two great canvases—as on a well-known etching in *The Disasters of War*—he might have written "Yo lo vi" (I saw this).

Goya's keen interest in everyday incidents had already inspired many drawings and the panels illustrating the capture of the highwayman Maragato. But perhaps he found more than enough to cope with in the riots of May 2nd and the tragic reprisals of the following day, since not until six years later did he commit them to canvas. Yet even then the scenes were obviously as fresh and vivid in his memory as if they had just taken place. Meanwhile, of course, he had drawn and etched his *Disasters of War* (which he withheld from publication), so that by 1814 he had accumulated a mass of firsthand documentary material relating to war. Out of a vast repertory of atrocities and heroism he then built up this unforgettable pair of canvases, a synthesis of all he had seen and heard in the war years.

First *The Charge of the Mamelukes*, in which the fury of battle is rendered by Goya with a like fury. No classical composition here, no carefully plotted lines of force, no axes, center points, etc. A wild tangle of men and horses swirls across the canvas, the horses panic-stricken, rearing this way and that, the men cutting each other down in blind savagery. There are no heroes in this murderous confusion; only the horde counts, a horde of Spaniards massed like the grips of a vice round Murat's mamelukes. On all sides planes drop away in depth without a break.

Their density is such that we feel there is no way out of the maelstrom—an impression intensified by the foreshortened figures in the foreground, whom we might almost reach out and touch. The weird impasto of colors might have been strewn over the canvas by a man beside himself with rage. Slashed with tints chosen for their violence and nothing else, horses and men are unlike anything on earth. The brushwork is so furious as to bring out only the bare essentials and make the picture as a whole strike like a whiplash on our nerves.

The revolt of May 2nd in Madrid and the guerilla warfare that then flared up all over Spain have this in common with the French Revolution: the people played the leading part and became aware for the first time of their collective strength. In both cases an angry mob rose up as one man, unled and virtually unarmed, and held its own against a strong, well-organized army. The people's rise to power had already been hinted at in the pictures Goya painted for the Academy of San Fernando in 1793. Thereafter he seemed to fall back exclusively on the individual, both in his portraits and drawings, and only under the stimulus of war did the masses reappear in his work, handled more powerfully than ever now and frequently reverted to in his last years. After *The Charge of the Mamelukes* and *The Shootings of May Third* came—to cite but a few examples—many etchings in *The Disasters of War* (where for the first time the expression "cannon fodder" takes on its full meaning), the crowd scenes in *The Tauromachia*, the congregation in *The Last Communion of St Joseph of Calasanz*, the Quinta del Sordo murals and the four lithographs known as *The Bulls of Bordeaux*.

As for the companion piece, *The Shootings of May Third*, this is easily the most dramatic historical painting ever made, though its scope far exceeds the traditional bounds of the classic *tableau d'histoire*. After the tumultuous scene of actual battle, in which broad daylight and the frenzy of hand-to-hand fighting

THE SHOOTINGS OF MAY THIRD, 1808, AT MADRID (1814). (104½ × 135½ ")
PRADO, MADRID.

made death almost a trivial matter, Goya now chose the most terrible moment of all, a split second before the resounding volley of the firing-squad, as the guns are leveled on a quaking group of unfortunates. In the dead of night, lit up by the bleak light of a huge lantern, this interminable instant of hushed suspense reaches an unbearable degree of agonizing tension.

The picture is an overwhelming revelation of barbarity. Tradition has it that, among many similar episodes, Goya represented the execution, shortly before daybreak, of forty-three Spanish patriots on the hill of Príncipe Pío just outside Madrid. But neither time, place nor date really matter; they are obliterated by this inspired vision of a tragedy whose every detail burns into the memory. First the blind wall of human backs formed by the soldiers shouldering their rifles, whose steely barrels flash in the lamplight; their sturdy legs planted wide apart, strictly parallel, outlined with thick black strokes of the brush; then, towering up in full light against this solid block of faceless gunmen, the helpless, pallid figure of a man flinging up his arms in a gesture—one that recurs in many works by Goya—that might either be despair or defiance and is probably both. Also the crazy-quilt of hands and clenched fists among the sprawling dead and those who are about to die; some with their faces buried in their hands so as not to see, others with their eyes starting out of their heads at what they cannot help but see. Finally the whole tonality of the picture which everywhere varies in keeping with the composition and intensifies the effect. Here, even more than in *The Charge of the Mamelukes*, Goya lets himself go and splashes on his colors in a frenzy; the blood of the dead seems to have been smeared on with the fingers, while some of the faces are barely sketched in. For sheer power and spontaneity it would be difficult to find another painting to compare with this.

Beside these two monumental paintings, inspired by the uprising in Madrid, stand two other war pictures, but so much smaller in size, so brightly, freshly colored, that the contrast is symbolic. In these we get a glimpse of mountaineers in an outlying region of Spain busy preparing munitions for the insurgents. The small figures, vibrant patches of pure color, go about their tasks in a delightful landscape of green hills and leafy trees. The very titles are a grim reminder of the guerilla warfare that had broken out all over Spain: *The Bullet-Makers* and *The Powder-Grinders in the Sierra de Tardienta* (Escorial).

A great many portraits of various kinds date from the war years. After that of Ferdinand VII in 1808 came two other equestrian portraits: *The Duke of Wellington* in 1812 (Wellington Collection, London) and *General Palafox* (Prado). But none of these works rises above a rather half-hearted drabness, and try as he might, Goya never produced anything comparable to the equestrian portraits of Titian and Velazquez.

Several portraits of near relations, however, call for special mention, above all those of his grandson Mariano. While there is no known portrait of his son Xavier as a child, and even his wife Josefa, a shy, self-effacing woman, cannot be positively identified in any work by Goya, he painted little Mariano twice in the space of three or four years. First about 1810, with his favorite toy, a small cart he pulls along behind him on a string (Collection of the Marquis of Larios, Malaga); this portrait is similar to the pictures of children made in 1788-1791. Next, in 1813, with an amusing hat on his head and a roll of music in his hand (Collection of the Duke of Alburquerque, Madrid). Two other works of the same period complete this set of children's portraits—always of boys, be it noted—, all wrapped in an air of wistful tenderness: in 1810 young *Victor Guye*, nephew of the French general Nicolas Guye (Harding Collection, New York) and, about 1813, young *Pepito Costa y Bonnell*, grandson of the Duchess of Alba's private doctor (Mellon Collection, Pittsburgh). (It is a matter of regret that General Hugo, whose sons Eugène and Victor were staying with him in Madrid in 1811, did not take the cue from his friend Nicolas Guye—had he done so we should now have a portrait by Goya of Victor Hugo as a child.)

THE POWDER-GRINDERS IN THE SIERRA DE TARDIENTA, CA. 1811.
(12½ × 20½″) ON WOOD. CASITA DEL PRINCIPE, PALACE OF THE ESCORIAL.

Everywhere in Goya's work, whether paintings, drawings or etchings, landscape plays second fiddle to the human element and dwindles to a mere backdrop in the tapestry cartoons, the seven decorative paintings for the Alameda de Osuna and the portraits (e.g. those of the Marchioness of Pontejos, La Tirana, the Duchess of Alba). There are exceptions, however, and under Velazquez' influence a distinct emphasis is laid on landscape in such cartoons as *The Washerwomen* and *The Tobacco Guard*. In the landscapes of some portraits he goes even farther in the way of blurred, misty effects. Then, from about 1800 on, the conventional backdrops almost completely disappear. Of all Goya's paintings only *The Fiesta of San Isidro* (Prado) and the two companion pictures at the Escorial, *The Powder-Grinders* and *The Bullet-Makers in the Sierra de Tardienta*, can properly be called "landscapes." The latter two, in particular, show nature in the raw in a mountainous setting under a limpid Castilian sky.

Also dating from 1810 are the portraits of the parents of Goya's daughter-in-law: *Don Martín de Goicoechea* and *Doña Juana Galarza* (Collection of the Marquis of Casa-Torres, Madrid), whose bourgeois placidity leaves nothing to be desired.

Four other portraits stand out from this period. In 1811 came the very fine *Don Juan Antonio Llorente* (Kaiser Friedrich Museum, Berlin), a well-known Bonapartist, who, after supervising the suppression of the monastic orders in Spain, wrote a famous *History of the Inquisition*. This was followed by three exquisitely mellow portraits of women: *Doña Sabasa García* (National Gallery, Washington) and two of the actress *Antonia Zárate* (one is in the Otto Beit Collection, London).

In these years great changes took place in Goya's private life. In 1812 his wife died and at sixty-six he found himself utterly alone in his house in the Calle Valverde, Madrid, Xavier and his young wife having moved into their own home in 1806. There now took place a division of property between father and son, and for this purpose an inventory of the family assets was drawn up. This document, one of the most precious we have in connection with Goya, was brought to light by Mr Sánchez Cantón, who first published it. Not only does it prove that the family was very comfortably off but, most important of all, it enumerates the paintings and prints in Goya's possession at the time, all of which were made over to Xavier *en bloc*, together with the house and the library. It seems extraordinary that Goya could so readily part with the very things that, as an artist, he must have treasured most, yet part with them he did—no less than 80 canvases, 75 by his own hand, as well as several print collections including works by Rembrandt, Wouwerman and Piranesi. A special interest attaches to this group of paintings in that, at the time, these constituted precisely the work no one had asked him to do; he painted them on his own initiative, as the fancy took him. Only two portraits figure among them:

one of the *Duchess of Alba* (in black, dated 1797) and one of the well-known torero *Pedro Romero*. Next come five religious pictures, which are now lost, and five allegorical scenes of little or no value. Then the six panels already mentioned illustrating the capture of the bandit Maragato. And, lastly, a whole gallery of new and extraordinary works: *The Colossus* (Prado), for example, which may safely be dated to the war years (1808-1812) and in which Goya's obsession with the gigantic first appears, and above all *The Water-Carrier* and *The Knife-Grinder* (Budapest Museum) and twelve war pictures (eight of them

◄   THE MONK'S VISIT, CA. 1810. (15¾ × 12½")
COLLECTION OF THE MARCHIONESS OF LA ROMANA, MADRID.

THE PEST-HOUSE, CA. 1810. (12½ × 22")
COLLECTION OF THE MARCHIONESS OF LA ROMANA, MADRID.

99

now owned by the Marchioness of La Romana, Madrid). *The Water-Carrier* and *The Knife-Grinder* are companion pieces and suggest that Goya was toying with the idea of a series of pictures relating to trades and occupations. The others, though plunging us again into the thick of war, spare us much of its horror, and among the eight canvases in the collection of the Marchioness of La Romana we find *The Pest-House*, one of Goya's greatest masterpieces. Under these gloomy vaults the air is heavy and fetid, reeking of disease. A stroke of bold originality is the garish light flooding in from a window at the back, filtering through the murky atmosphere and lighting up a mass of ghostly figures from behind. The other scenes are rendered in a narrow range of blacks, burnt siennas and dark browns, with eery shafts of light striking through the gloom. Here a man stabs a half-naked woman at the entrance of a cave; there a pack of bandits are stripping their victim; elsewhere a monk and a woman confabulate under cover of darkness—and so it goes. The unity and variety of these small pictures, as somber as the dark doings they but half unveil!

As for the remaining canvases listed in this inventory, we find two very similar *Majas on a Balcony*—that most "Goyesque" of themes, reminiscent of the *Young Girls* and *Old Women* in Lille Museum—and, a new departure in Goya's work, twelve still lifes. Among the latter may certainly be included the two Prado canvases of turkey and fowl that Goya is said to have presented to friends as Christmas gifts, and above all the *Still Life with a Sheep's Head* (Louvre) and the *Still Life with Salmon* (Oskar Reinhart Collection, Winterthur). Mr Charles Sterling has rightly described these brutally forthright works as landmarks in the history of the still life. Goya took up the torch where Rembrandt, with his *Flayed Ox*, had left it, and at the same time anticipated both the realism of the 19th century and Soutine's expressionism.

Hopes ran high when Ferdinand VII was restored to the throne in 1814, but the young king was quick to dash them all. With the war over and internal dissensions apparently at an end, an era of peace, justice and prosperity seemed in the offing. The liberal Constitution of 1812 dazzled the eyes of Spaniards like a symbolic flame of their new-won freedom, but they waited in vain for it to be proclaimed and put into effect. Swayed by a handful of reactionary fanatics, Ferdinand VII not only repudiated the new constitution but launched into a despotic policy of vengeance and repression. Even before entering Madrid in May 1814, he issued an infamous decree against the liberals, then another against all "collaborators" with the French; he reinstituted the monastic orders and, in July, the Inquisition. Six bitter years of war and revolution had been to no avail, and Spain entered on another six years of oppression and obscurantism.

Stepping as cautiously as ever, Goya quietly continued performing his duties as Court Painter and on July 8, 1814, took part in the reception of the king at the Academy. Severe penalties were being meted out to those who had fraternized with the French, but somehow Goya came through unscathed; he retained his official post and again drew his salary, which had been cut off during the war. But this was only a hollow show of royal favor; Goya received no commissions from the king and seldom appeared at Court. Probably he was only too glad to step aside in favor of Vicente Lopez, who rapidly ingratiated himself and was kept busy filling orders from the Court and the aristocracy—to the great detriment of Spanish art!

As he watched events from close at hand and followed the government policy of stern repression, disgust again got the better of Goya. He saw his closest friends driven into exile, Meléndez Valdés and Moratín among others, while the actor Isidoro Máiquez, whose portrait he had painted in pre-war days, was thrown into prison in 1814, then released but given no peace thereafter by the police and the Inquisition until finally he was banished from Madrid and died insane in 1820. It is reckoned that from 1814 to 1820 some 12,000 Spaniards accused of French sympathies—*afrancesamiento*—were tracked down by the political police and finally exiled for life. Goya himself came under a cloud in 1814. Godoy's property having been confiscated, the Grand Inquisitor made a great stir over five "obscene" paintings found in his collections, two of which were the famous *Maja Nude* and *Maja Clothed*. In May 1815 the prosecutor general of the Inquisition summoned Goya to appear before the Tribunal and admit or deny authorship of the two pictures. Though we hear nothing more of the matter—some influential friend having no doubt seen to it that the old painter was left in peace—it must have been obvious to Goya that there was nothing to hope for from Ferdinand VII. And the same patriotic fervor that had led him to etch the first sixty-five plates of *The Disasters of War* now inspired him with an extra set of fifteen etchings lampooning the new régime. Unpublished in his lifetime, these works leave no doubt as to Goya's feelings: foreign invasion and bad government lead to the same terrorism, one destroying national independence, the other crushing out freedom and human dignity.

A number of drawings arranged in logical sequence by Goya himself form an indictment of the times contemporaneous with the last etchings of *The Disasters*. These show *encorozados* (the accused as they appear before the Tribunal of the Inquisition wearing the tall cap known as the *coroza*) and prisoners chained in their cells or undergoing torture. The captions voice Goya's indignation at these inhuman practices and his hope of better things to come—*Horrible to see, Death would be better, Time will have its say, Wake up, innocent!, You will soon be free*. Great art in themselves, these drawings are all the greater for Goya's courage in putting his art to the service of a noble cause.

From now till 1816 he painted several portraits, notably those of the *Duke of San Carlos* (Oficinas del Canal Imperial, Saragossa) and *Don José Luis de Munárriz* (Academy of San Fernando, Madrid). The two well-known self-portraits in the Prado and the Academy of San Fernando date from 1815—a wonderful head, wonderful features, into which we can read all the lassitude and sufferings of mankind. A lingering coquetry has led him to make himself younger and better-looking than he must have been. Why? Or better, for whom? He had been living in solitude and retirement since his wife's death. Had another woman come into his life? We know practically nothing about the start of his relations with Doña Leocadia Weiss—his housekeeper and a distant relative—nor has it ever been proved who was really the father of little Rosario, to whom Goya was so fondly attached at the end of his life in Bordeaux. When the child was born in 1814, Doña Leocadia was only twenty-six and had apparently been separated from her husband Don Isidro Weiss since 1811. Some profess to be shocked at the idea that Goya, nearing seventy, should keep a young mistress, but no one is shocked at Goethe's having done so. While nothing can be said for certain, there is no particular reason for rejecting what seems very probable and even natural. Goya's attachment to Doña Leocadia, furthermore, would explain why he never went to live with his children after his wife's death, though his age and infirmities made it necessary for him to have someone to look after him.

In 1816 he painted portraits of the *Duchess of Abrantes* (Collection of the Marquis del Valle de Orizaba, Madrid) and her brother the *Duke of Osuna* (Prado), children of his former patrons. But whether out of ill-humor or sheer weariness with these society portraits, the work, though not scamped, was distinctly mediocre, and from now on the aristocracy dropped Goya for good and turned to Vicente Lopez for its portraits.

For his own amusement and pleasure Goya reverted to a theme that was an old favorite with him—bullfighting—and made *The Tauromachia*, his tribute to Spain's great toreadors. He combined etching and aquatint to illustrate some of the most celebrated *faenas* and *cogidas* he himself had witnessed: the extravagant antics of Martincho at Saragossa, the tragic death of the Alcade de Torrejón at Madrid, Mariano Ceballos bullfighting on horseback, and above all the feats of the idols of his youth, Pedro Romero and Pepe Hillo, whose death in 1801 had plunged the whole of Spain into mourning. In these prints, an admirable synthesis of a spectacle unique for color and movement, Goya captured straight from the life all the thrilling beauty of the three participants: the animal, the man dancing round him, the seething crowd of spectators.

From 1817 to 1824 he lived more or less withdrawn from the world, accepting only very occasional commissions. One of these, in 1817, forced him to make the long journey to Seville, where he made to order a rather disappointing picture of *Sts Justa and Rufina* for the cathedral. To about the same period may be dated the mysterious, monumental *Junta of the Philippines*, now in the museum at Castres (the preliminary sketch is in the Kaiser Friedrich Museum, Berlin). Here the vast perspective vista and bold lighting almost crowd out the assembly of dignitaries presided over, presumably, by Ferdinand VII. The deliberate disproportion between this austere high-ceilinged assembly-room and the rows of tiny figures along the bare walls creates an atmosphere of uneasy, indefinable expectation. Thus is an ordinary conference—probably of the Royal Company of the Philippines—transposed by the wizardry of Goya's brush into a thing of pure expression.

CHRIST IN THE GARDEN OF OLIVES, 1819. ($18\frac{1}{2} \times 13\frac{3}{4}$") ON WOOD. ▶
ESCUELAS PÍAS DE SAN ANTÓN, MADRID.

Full of dark power and mystic longings, *The Last Communion of St Joseph of Calasanz* (Escuelas Pías de San Antón, Madrid) is one of Goya's crowning masterpieces. Commissioned and executed in 1819 for the church in which it remains to this day, the picture displays as beautiful a scale of blacks and somber greys as ever issued from his palette. The priest's chasuble, the ecstatic face of the saint bathed in a supernatural light, his clasped hands, the kneeling congregation and an inrush of daylight through the high arches on the right—all this produces an effect of intense religious emotion, conspicuously absent in Goya's work. Though a prolific painter of devotional pictures, he had always held aloof from the mysteries of the faith. Here, for the first time, we feel him touched to the heart, identifying himself with the worshippers in the background, who kneel in prayer with lowered eyelids. Also in the Escuelas Pías, a small *Christ in the Garden of Olives*—whose outflung arms recall the central figure in *The Shootings of May Third*—vouches for this onset of genuine religious fervor. To call it a conversion would certainly be going too far, since nothing tangible came of it afterwards. But when we remember the spell of illness to which Goya nearly succumbed late in 1819, at seventy-three, we can readily imagine the frame of mind in which he must have tackled these amazing pictures. We can picture him, too, musing over the memories of his early childhood spent in the Escuelas Pías of Saragossa. Perhaps he saw himself once again, like the choir-boys in his picture, filled with awe at the mysterious ritual of the Communion. His health, now giving way, inclined him to a vague search for something to lean on and believe in and, his mind filled with an old man's vague apprehensions, he painted the image of a dying man's salvation: the Eucharist.

THE LAST COMMUNION OF ST JOSEPH OF CALASANZ, 1819. (98¼ × 70¾ ") ►
ESCUELAS PÍAS DE SAN ANTÓN, MADRID.

THE LAST COMMUNION OF ST JOSEPH OF CALASANZ (DETAIL), 1819.
ESCUELAS PÍAS DE SAN ANTÓN, MADRID.

THE LAST COMMUNION OF ST JOSEPH OF CALASANZ (DETAIL), 1819.
ESCUELAS PÍAS DE SAN ANTÓN, MADRID.

Yet the year 1819 had begun auspiciously enough. In February he bought a country place just across the Manzanares, not far from the Segovia Bridge: some twenty-five acres of land with a villa on it, which he had renovated and enlarged. This has always been known as the *Quinta del Sordo* (the Deaf Man's House) and it has always been taken for granted that the name originated with Goya. The Marquis del Saltillo has recently proved, however, that such is not the case, and that by a curious coincidence this name had been given to a neighboring estate long before Goya bought his house. Whether in buying it Goya simply desired to make a safe investment or wanted a quiet place to live in with his new family, is hard to say. It is a matter of record that he had the house enlarged, which implies that he did not intend to live there alone. When he actually moved in is not known, nor do we know exactly when he decorated the walls with the so-called *pinturas negras*.

It was also in February 1819, through his friend Cardano who had just set up the first lithographic plant in Madrid, that Goya initiated himself into the new technique—proof of his enquiring mind, always eager to explore newly opened byways of art. The greater freedom allowed by the lithographic process—much more direct than etching—enchanted him at once. From now till 1824 he made ten lithographs in Madrid, and after that another thirteen in France, among them his famous *Bulls of Bordeaux*. In lithography as in other fields he innovated boldly and impressed on the stone the full vitality of his linework. Beside Goya, every other artist of the day who tried his hand at lithography cuts a pale figure. He alone, in his very first attempts, made it yield the striking effects that justified his using it.

TWO WOMEN LAUGHING, CA. 1820. (49¼ × 26″) PRADO, MADRID. ▶
(MURAL FROM THE QUINTA DEL SORDO)

III

FANTASTIC VISION (AL AQUELARRE), CA. 1820. (48½ × 104″)
PRADO, MADRID. (MURAL FROM THE QUINTA DEL SORDO)

Before migrating to France in 1824, Goya painted three of his finest portraits of men, beautifully free and frank in treatment: in 1819, the architect *Don Juan Antonio Cuervo* (Museum of Art, Cleveland); in 1820, another architect, his good friend *Tiburcio Pérez* (Metropolitan Museum, New York); and in 1823 (or perhaps 1820), *Don Ramón Satue* (Rijksmuseum, Amsterdam). The self-portrait showing him as a convalescent in the arms of Dr Arrieta seems to have disappeared. A work similar in style dates probably from 1819: *The Forge* (Frick Collection, New York), whose vigorous handling recalls *The Knife-Grinder* (Budapest Museum).

In 1820 a politico-military mutiny led by an army officer, Colonel Rafael Riego, developed into a nation-wide revolt and in March Ferdinand VII was compelled to restore the Constitution. This was a red-letter day for Spain and Goya joyfully commemorated it in three allegorical drawings. The first of these, *Divina Libertad* (Divine Liberty), strangely resembles his *Christ in the Garden of Olives* of 1819, but here the focus of interest is the beatific smile with which this curious figure welcomes the dawn of freedom. As for the other two drawings, powerful studies in chiaroscuro, one shows the forces of darkness and oppression falling back before the radiant figure of Truth holding the Constitution (this is entitled *Lux ex tenebris*); the other shows darkness receding behind a set of truly balanced scales. After this there could be no doubt as to Goya's political views. On April 4, 1820, he made his last appearance at the Academy, attending the special session at which allegiance was solemnly sworn to the Constitution.

Little is known about his life during the next three years, but to this period belong two major works, extraordinary

PILGRIMAGE TO THE MIRACULOUS FOUNTAIN OF SAN ISIDRO, CA. 1820. (48½ × 104½″) PRADO, MADRID. (MURAL FROM THE QUINTA DEL SORDO)

creations, each unique of its kind: the Black Paintings in the Quinta del Sordo and the *Disparates* etchings. The illness of 1819 brought about an upheaval in Goya's mental life quite as violent as those produced by his previous illness in 1793 and by war in 1808. The sublime yet monstrous phantasmagoria of his dreams haunted his waking hours, and these he recorded on the walls of his country home in fourteen paintings, the weirdest, most mysterious known to art. It was a vast undertaking, paralleled only by the frescos in San Antonio de la

FANTASTIC VISION (AL AQUELARRE), DETAIL. CA. 1820. PRADO, MADRID. (MURAL FROM THE QUINTA DEL SORDO)

PILGRIMAGE TO THE MIRACULOUS FOUNTAIN OF SAN ISIDRO (DETAIL), CA. 1820. PRADO, MADRID. (MURAL FROM THE QUINTA DEL SORDO)

Florida, but in it we have a completely different world, a world of rich black, pure white, glowing ochres and sudden slashes of raw color. Goya gave no names to these strange pictures but we can recognize themes from earlier works: nocturnal gatherings of witches and wizards, a procession, a pilgrimage, a street-fight, repulsive old men and women, alluring young *manolas*. Everything in the Black Paintings is sinister, furtive, disquieting; Goya had welcomed into his home "the monsters born when reason sleeps," the monsters of his *Caprices*, and accepted them as his familiars. Yet there is nothing of dejection or defeat in these works; on the contrary, they proclaim an indomitable spirit, a worshipper of color and poetry in *Al Aquelarre* and *The Pilgrimage to the Miraculous Fountain of San Isidro*, a dreamer of horrific visions in *Saturn* and the *Aquelarre*. The creative imagination that had gone into *The Caprices* some thirty years before is here intensified a hundred-fold; beyond this limit lies the unimaginable.

Inspired by the same "black" visions, the twenty-two etchings of the *Disparates*, or *Proverbs* (1820-1824), show the same obsession with the gigantic. In them Goya kept to the technique of *The Caprices*, combining aquatint with the etched line to even finer effect. Lying outside space and time, though forms still are human, the *Disparates*—like Gérard de Nerval's *Aurélia* of a later day—evoke that Descent into Hell which a man can describe only once in a lifetime.

The interlude of liberalism that Ferdinand VII had reluctantly granted Spain was short-lived. In 1823, with the blessing of the continental powers after the Congress of Verona (and chiefly at the instigation of Chateaubriand, French plenipotentiary at the Congress), a French army under the Duke of Angoulême came to the rescue of absolutism in Spain. Meeting with little opposition, it had restored Ferdinand VII to the throne by August. Spaniards paid dearly for their three years of constitutional government; the new régime was more oppressive, more vindictive than ever. Even the Duke of Angoulême was shocked and addressed a protest to the king: "A fortnight has passed since Your Majesty regained the sovereign power, and so far it has been signalized by one long series of arbitrary edicts and arrests, with the result that there is growing discontent and consternation among your subjects." To a man the liberals fled the country or went into hiding. Goya grew anxious; trial proofs of his *Disasters of War* were already being circulated and his studio was full of incriminating drawings. Fearing a possible confiscation of his property, he made haste to transfer the ownership of the Quinta del Sordo to his grandson

PILGRIMAGE TO THE MIRACULOUS FOUNTAIN OF SAN ISIDRO (DETAIL), CA. 1820. PRADO, MADRID. (MURAL FROM THE QUINTA DEL SORDO)

TWO OLD MEN EATING PORRIDGE, CA. 1820. (20¾ × 33½")
PRADO, MADRID. (MURAL FROM THE QUINTA DEL SORDO)

The so-called Black Paintings, fourteen in number, all of them now in
the Prado, once covered the walls of the Quinta del Sordo, the house
Goya bought in 1819 across the Manzanares from Madrid. Painted in
oils directly on the walls, which had been prepared with a thin coating of
lime, they were only preserved thanks to the enlightened initiative of the
German banker Baron Erlanger, last owner of the house before it was
demolished, who had them detached from the wall and transferred on to
canvas in 1873. Exhibited in Paris at the 1878 World's Fair, they passed
unnoticed and were finally given to the Prado. The most original, freely
handled works of Goya's maturity, they are like an eruption from the
depths of his soul, an outburst of dark forces that lands us squarely in
the Irrational, whether we like it or not. Yet forms in themselves have
changed little since the days of the tapestry cartoons, while everywhere
are reminiscences of *The Caprices*, the Florida frescos, and even the seven
Alameda de Osuna paintings of 1787. Here, as in all Goya's work, we feel
an immutable foundation of imaginative power and technical virtuosity.

Mariano, now seventeen. But things went from bad to worse; Riego was hanged in November and in January 1824 military tribunals were set up in the provincial capitals and empowered to try all persons who had even spoken in favor of the now abolished constitution. Goya promptly went into hiding—a fact firmly established by Mr Sánchez Cantón—in the home of an Aragonese friend, Don José Duaso y Latre (whose portrait he painted). A decree of amnesty was signed on May 1 and the very next day, obviously in a hurry to get away, Goya applied to the king for permission to "take the waters" at Plombières in France. In June he crossed the frontier, heading for Bordeaux and Paris. He started out alone; it is now known that Leocadia Weiss and her two children joined him at Bordeaux in September. Perhaps before leaving he painted the portrait of *Doña María Martínez de Puga* (Frick Collection, New York); of all his works this one comes nearest to Manet's style.

Goya was seventy-eight when he arrived at Bordeaux in June 1824 but his mind and eyes were as alert as ever. His old friend Moratín, living in exile at Bordeaux with Manuel Silvela, welcomed him there. "Goya has come," he wrote. "He is an old man, stone deaf, doesn't know a word of French and hasn't even got a servant with him (though no one needs one more than he does). But he's happy to be here and eager to see all the sights." Goya went on almost at once to Paris, where he lived from June 30 to September 1, lodging at 5, rue Marivaux. In Paris he associated chiefly with Spanish refugees, in particular Joaquín Ferrer and his wife (whose portraits he painted).

If the records of the Paris police are to be trusted, Goya spent most of his time indoors, and "when he went out it was only to see the sights of the city and roam the streets." He may well have visited the Louvre and the Luxembourg Gallery and would surely have looked in at the Salon, which opened on August 25. In it figured Delacroix's *Massacres at Chios*, Ingres'

Vow of Louis XIII, Lawrence's *Portrait of the Duke of Richelieu* and above all landscapes by Constable and Bonington, in which Goya must have found a striking confirmation of the methods he had used twenty-five years earlier in the frescos at San Antonio de la Florida and, in 1811, in his two small impressionist landscapes of the Sierra de Tardienta. This first revelation of contemporary painting abroad augured well for his own fame and he must have realized it. Yet during the two months he spent in Paris no one, aside from a few personal friends, all Spaniards, seems to have been aware of his presence there, nor did he know that his *Caprices* had already attracted attention, that Delacroix had copied several of them and was planning "some caricatures in the Goya manner." Nor did he have any inkling that a few months later a publisher in Paris was to bring out ten rather muddled copies of his *Caprices* in the form of lithographs. As a matter of fact, by the time the French romantics were discovering and admiring *The Caprices*, Goya himself had moved on to the Black Paintings, the *Disparates* and pure expressionism. The young romantics of 1824 were all for monarchy and Catholicism and their god was Chateaubriand. In the eyes of an old liberal like Goya, Chateaubriand was responsible for the restoration of absolute monarchy in Spain and, as such, detestable.

Returning to Bordeaux in September, Goya was joined there by Leocadia Weiss and her two children, and they set up house together. There he spent the last years of his life, except for two brief trips to Madrid in 1826 and 1827. He saw only a few friends in the Spanish colony; in their company he found relief from his nostalgia for his native land. Though half blind, he went on working indefatigably, always trying out new ideas, never reverting to an earlier style. "Goya is quite full of himself *(muy arrogantillo)*," his friend Moratín wrote in a letter.

PORTRAIT OF DON JOSÉ PÍO DE MOLINA, 1827-1828. $(23\frac{1}{2} \times 19\frac{1}{2}'')$
OSKAR REINHART COLLECTION, WINTERTHUR.

"He is painting away as hard as he can, never stopping to correct what he has painted." He now made portraits of *Moratín* (Bilbao Museum), *Santiago Galos* (Barnes Collection, Merion, Pa.) and *Don Juan Bautista Muguiro* (Prado), gratified to find, at the age of over eighty, that his hand had lost none of its cunning.

Life with Doña Leocadia was not all plain sailing, but Goya had the consolation of having his little Rosario, now ten, always at his side. He taught her drawing and predicted brilliant things for her (actually he greatly overrated her talents). Together they started painting miniatures on ivory and Goya boasted to his friend Ferrer that they had produced no less than forty of these, which, so he said, "came much nearer the style of Velazquez than that of Mengs." From Paris Ferrer must have reported the success of *The Caprices* and suggested that new copies should be printed off, as we find Goya vetoing the idea; he no longer had the copper plates, he replied, and did not feel like making copies of his own work, he had "better things to do." He had just made his remarkable set of lithographs, *The Bulls of Bordeaux,* and hoped to sell them anonymously in Paris. But there was no demand for them; what people liked were *The Caprices.* So he gave up the idea of trying to sell and worked on his own, turning out a great many drawings, some anecdotal, some visionary and fantastic. He now developed an addiction for circuses, fairs, guillotine executions, and performing animals; he also drew a series of *Madmen* with all his old sureness of design.

During his last visit to Madrid in 1827, where Vicente Lopez had succeeded him as First Court Painter, he made a final portrait of Mariano, whose boyish features reflect the same willfulness and virility as those of his grandfather. But returning to Bordeaux Goya did not remain idle and again produced a work that takes us completely by surprise: *The Milkmaid of Bordeaux* (Prado), whose girlish figure and dreamy, faraway

THE MILKMAID OF BORDEAUX, 1826-1827. $(29\frac{1}{2} \times 26\frac{1}{4}'')$
PRADO, MADRID.

One of Goya's last works and one of his tenderest—a pretty girl with
parted lips and dreamy eyes, languorous and pensive. After so many
fierce and somber works born of tragic experiences, Goya revels for the
last time in the whole scale of greens and blues, luminous and translucent.
Here, as Sánchez Cantón writes, he had "a presentiment of Impressionism."

gaze embody all the melancholy languor of youth. This was his farewell to color and beauty; fingers of light steal over the hair and caress the shoulders, dividing tones and shimmering through a haze of tender blues and greens. Renoir was still unborn, yet Impressionism could already boast one of its greatest masters.

Goya's last canvas was a portrait: *Don José Pío de Molina* (Oskar Reinhart Collection, Winterthur). After the poetry and grace of *The Milkmaid of Bordeaux* came now the fierce Goya of old, slashing the canvas with his brush, building up features in rugged planes of color applied with easy mastery. At eighty-two he was still going so strong that one cannot help speculating on the works he might yet have created had death not intervened at last. Feeling unwell in March 1828, he took to his bed and got up for the last time, joyfully, to welcome his daughter-in-law and his grandson Mariano who had hastened to Bordeaux to be with him. Next morning he awoke half paralysed and died a few days later on April 16, 1828.

Today his ashes repose in the church of San Antonio de la Florida at Madrid, commended to the protection of the angels and the men and women of the people he painted on the ceiling above. No more fitting place of rest could have been chosen than this little church, whose dome enshrines one of his most perfect creations. The Florida frescos sum up everything painting had achieved in the past and anticipate everything it was to achieve in years to come. The Quinta del Sordo no longer exists and its wall paintings are now in the Prado; they evoke that night-side of things which is part and parcel of human nature. But it is only one side, from which we may turn away to find the other, the high noon of sunlit things such as Goya imagined and so gloriously portrayed it in the church of San Antonio de la Florida.

SELECTED BIBLIOGRAPHY

EXHIBITIONS

INDEX OF NAMES

CONTENTS

SELECTED BIBLIOGRAPHY

I. Bibliographical Works

G. Estrada, *Bibliografía de Goya*, Mexico City 1940. — A. Ruiz Cabriada, *Aportación a una bibliografía de Goya*, Madrid 1946.

II. Goya's Letters

Up to the present time only about a quarter of Goya's extant letters have been published; a complete edition (some 220 letters) is now in preparation in Spain. Such letters as have already been published, either in whole or in part, will be found in the following works: Count of La Viñaza, *Goya, su tiempo, su vida, sus obras*, Madrid 1887. — A. L. Mayer, *Goya's Briefe an Martin Zapater*, Antiquariat Rosenthal I, Munich 1915. — A. de Beruete, vol. I: *Goya, pintor de retratos*; vol. II: *Goya, composiciones y figuras*; vol. III: *Goya, grabador*, Madrid 1916-1918. — V. von Loga, *Francisco de Goya*, Berlin 1903. — A. L. Mayer, *Francisco de Goya*, Munich 1923. — F. Zapater y Gomez, *Goya, noticias biográficas*, Madrid 1924. — G. Diaz-Plaja, *Epistolario de Goya*, Mentora, Barcelona 1928.

III. Catalogues

1. Paintings

C. Yriarte, *Goya*, Plon, Paris 1867. — E. Tormo y Monzo, *Las pinturas de Goya*, Tello, Madrid 1902. — A. L. Mayer, *Goya*, Munich 1923. — X. Desparmet Fitz-Gerald, *L'œuvre peint de Goya*, De Nobele, Paris 1950.

2. Etchings, Lithographs and Drawings

E. Piot, *Catalogue raisonné de l'œuvre gravé de Goya*, preface by Théophile Gautier, in *Le Cabinet de l'Amateur et de l'Antiquaire*, Paris 1842. — P. Lefort, *Essai de catalogue raisonné de l'œuvre gravé et lithographié de Francisco Goya*, in *Gazette des Beaux-Arts*, Paris 1877. — J. Hofmann, *Francisco de Goya, Katalog seines graphischen Werkes*, Vienna 1907. — L. Delteil, *Le peintre graveur illustré*, vols. XIV and XV, Paris 1922. — M. Velasco y Aguirre, *Grabados y litografías de Goya*, Espasa Calpe, Madrid 1928. — C. Dodgson, *Los Desastres de la Guerra*, Oxford University Press 1933. — H. B. Wehle, *Fifty Drawings by Francisco Goya*, Metropolitan Museum, New York 1938. — A. Malraux, *Dessins de Goya au Musée du Prado*, with a tentative catalogue by P. Gassier, Skira, Geneva 1947. — F. J. Sánchez Cantón, *Los Caprichos de Goya y sus dibujos preparatorios*, Instituto Amatller,

Barcelona 1949. — J. Camon Aznar, *Los Disparates de Goya y sus dibujos preparatorios*, Instituto Amatller, Barcelona 1951. — E. Lafuente Ferrari, *Los Desastres de la Guerra de Goya y sus dibujos preparatorios*, Instituto Amatller, Barcelona 1952. — J. Lopez Rey, *Goya's Caprichos*, Princeton University Press 1953. — F. J. Sánchez Cantón, *Los Dibujos de Fr. de Goya*, Museo del Prado, Madrid 1954.

IV. Monographs and Appraisals

Standard works for the study of Goya are: E. Lafuente Ferrari, *Antecedentes, coincidencias y influencias en el arte de Goya*, Madrid 1947 — F. J. Sánchez Cantón, *Vida y obras de Goya*, Peninsular, Madrid 1951.

1. 19th Century

T. Gautier, *Voyage en Espagne...*, pp. 127-137, Paris 1845. — C. Baudelaire, *Quelques caricaturistes étrangers*, in *Curiosités esthétiques*, Paris 1880 (article published in *Le Présent* in 1857). — L. Matheron, *Goya*, Paris 1858 (dedicated to Delacroix). — F. Zapater y Gomez, *Goya, noticias biográficas*, Saragossa 1868; reprinted Madrid 1924. — Count of La Viñaza, *Goya*, Madrid 1887. — Z. Araujo Sanchez, *Goya*, Madrid 1896.

2. 20th Century

V. von Loga, *Goya*, Berlin 1903. — A. F. Calvert, *Goya*, London 1908. — H. Stokes, *Goya*, London 1914. — J. Tild, *Goya*, Alcan, Paris 1921. — A. Salcedo y Ruiz, *La época de Goya*, Calleja, Madrid 1924. — J. Ezquerra del Bayo, *La Duquesa de Alba y Goya*, Ruiz Hnos, Madrid 1927. — J. de la Encina, *Goya en Zig-zag*, Espasa Calpe, Madrid 1928. — P. Paris, *Goya*, Plon, Paris 1928. — R. Gomez de la Serna, *Goya*, Atenea, Madrid 1928. — P. Frederix, *Goya*, L'Artisan du Livre, Paris 1928. — E. D'Ors, *L'Art de Goya*, Delagrave, Paris 1928. — E. D'Ors, *La Vie de Goya*, Gallimard, Paris 1928. — J. D'Elbée, *Le Sourd et le Muet* (Goya and Delacroix), Plon, Paris 1931. — C. Terrasse, *Goya*, Floury, Paris 1931. — G. Grappe, *Goya*, Plon, Paris 1937. — J. Adhémar, *Goya*, Tisné, Paris 1941. — J. Gudiol, *Goya*, Hyperion Press, New York 1941. — X. de Salas, *La Familia de Carlos IV*, Juventud, Barcelona 1944. — E. Lafuente Ferrari, « *El Dos de Mayo* » y « *Los Fusilamientos* », Juventud, Barcelona 1946. — J. Lopez Rey, *Goya y el mundo a su alrededor*, Buenos Aires 1947. — V. de Sambricio, *Tapices de Goya*, Madrid 1946-1948. — J. Lassaigne, *Goya*, Hypérion, Paris 1948. — F. D. Klingender, *Goya in the Democratic Tradition*, Sidgwick and Jackson, London 1948. — *Goya, Cinco estudios* (J. Camon Aznar, M. L. Caturla, E. Lafuente Ferrari, E. Sánchez Cantón, J. Subira), Diputación Provincial, Saragossa 1949. — J. Ortega y Gasset, *Papeles sobre Velazquez y Goya*, Revista de Occidente, Madrid 1950. — A. MAL-RAUX, *Saturne* (Essai sur Goya), Gallimard, Paris 1950. — A. VALLENTIN, *Goya*, Albin Michel, Paris 1951. — Marquis of SALTILLO, *Miscelanea Madrileña, histórica y artística; Goya en Madrid, su familia y allegados*, Madrid 1952.

V. Magazine Articles

Special numbers devoted to Goya: *Aragón*, No. 31, Saragossa, April 1928. — *La Esfera, Illustración Mundial*, No. 745, Madrid 1928. — *Boletín de la Sociedad Española de Excursiones*, Madrid 1928. — *Arte Español*, Madrid 1928. — *L'Art Vivant*, Paris, April 15, 1928. — *Artistica*, Paris, February 1930. — *Revista de Ideas Estéticas*, No. 15-16, Madrid 1946. — *Boletín de la Real Academia de la Historia*, Madrid 1946. — G. BRUNET, *L'œuvre de Francisco Goya*, in *Revue Universelle des Arts*, vol. VIII, pp. 450-453, 1858. — V. CARDERERA, *Goya, sa vie, ses dessins et ses eaux-fortes*, in *Gazette des Beaux-Arts*, 1860 (pp. 215-217) and 1863 (pp. 237-249). — J. CASSOU, *Goya*, in *L'Art et les Artistes*, 1926 (pp. 37-63). — MAC MAHON, *The Life of Goya*, in *The Arts*, 1926 (pp. 67-106). — M. GOMEZ MORENO, *Las crisis de Goya*, in *Revista de la Biblioteca*, Archivo y Museo del Ayuntamiento de Madrid, 1935. — J. ADHÉMAR, *Essai sur les débuts de l'influence de Goya en France au XIXᵉ siècle...*, in *Goya, Exposition de l'œuvre gravé...*, Bibliothèque Nationale, Paris 1935. — R. HUYGHE, *Musée de Castres, La série des Goya*, in *Bulletin des Musées de France*, November 1936. — C. STERLING, *Les Goya des collections de France*, in *Bulletin des Musées de France*, January 1938. — M. S. SORIA, *Agustín Esteve and Goya*, in *Art Bulletin*, Brown University, Providence, Rhode Island, September 1943. — F. J. SÁNCHEZ CANTÓN, *Como vivía Goya*, in *Archivo Español de Arte*, No. 74, Madrid 1946. — M. NUÑEZ DE ARENAS, *La suerte de Goya en Francia...*, in *Bulletin Hispanique*, No. 3, Bordeaux 1950. — J. CAMON AZNAR, *La estética de Goya en los Disparates*, in *Revista de Ideas Estéticas*, No. 35, Madrid 1951. — J. MILICUA, *Anotaciones al Goya, joven*, in *Paragone*, Florence, May 1954.

VI. First Editions of the Etchings and Lithographs

15 etchings from Velazquez and one from Carreño, printed by Goya, Madrid 1778. — *Los Caprichos* (80 etchings), about 240 copies, printed by Goya, Madrid 1799. — *La Tauromaquia* (33 etchings), printed by Goya, Madrid 1816. — *Les Taureaux de Bordeaux* (4 lithographs), 100 copies printed by Gaulon, Bordeaux 1825. — *Los Desastres de la Guerra* (80 etchings), 500 copies, Academy of San Fernando, Madrid 1863. — *Los Proverbios* (or *Disparates*) (22 etchings), 250 copies, Academy of San Fernando, Madrid 1864.

EXHIBITIONS

Galerie Espagnole, Musée Royal du Louvre, Paris (notice by Baron Taylor), 1838. — *Exhibition of Early Proofs of the Caprices*, Galerie Laffitte, Paris 1896. — *Works by Goya* (163 items), Madrid 1900. — Galerie Heinemann, Munich 1911. — *Exhibition of the Caprices and the Proverbs*, Keppel and Co., New York 1911. — *Paintings by Goya and El Greco*, Knoedler's, New York 1915. — *Goya's Etchings*, Ateneo, Madrid 1918. — *Exhibition of Modern Spanish Painting*, Palais des Beaux-Arts de la Ville de Paris, 1919. — *Spanish Drawings of the 18th and 19th Centuries* (69 drawings by Goya), Sociedad de Amigos de Arte, Madrid 1922. — *Prints*, Calcografía Nacional, Madrid 1927. — *Centenary Exhibition*, Prado, Madrid 1928. — *Exhibition of Goya's Drawings at the Prado* (472 drawings), Madrid 1928. — *Exhibition of the Black-and-White Work*, Sociedad de Amigos de Arte, Madrid 1928. — *Works from the Lazaro Collection*, Casa de Blanco y Negro, Madrid 1928. — Museo de Bellas Artes, Saragossa 1928. — *Spanish Paintings from El Greco to Goya*, Metropolitan Museum of Art, New York 1928. — Sociedad de Amigos de Arte, Madrid 1932. — *Engravings, Paintings, Tapestries and 110 Drawings*, Bibliothèque Nationale, Paris 1935. — *Paintings, Drawings, Prints*, Metropolitan Museum of Art, New York 1936. — *Paintings, Drawings, Prints*, Palace of Art, San Francisco 1937. — *Les Goya des collections de France*, Musée de l'Orangerie, Paris 1938. — *From El Greco to Goya*, Spanish Art Gallery, London 1938. — *The Masterpieces of the Prado* (22 pictures by Goya), Musée d'Art et d'Histoire, Geneva 1939. — Art Institute of Chicago, 1941. — Bicentenary Exhibition, Palacio de Oriente, Madrid 1946. — *Prints and Drawings*, National Library, Madrid 1946. — *Coppers and Books and Pamphlets about Goya*, Academy of San Fernando, Madrid 1946. — *Goya and French Art*, French Institute, Madrid 1946. — Wildenstein Gallery, New York 1950. — Bordeaux Museum, 1951. — Prado, Madrid 1951 (selection of works from the Bordeaux exhibition). — *From El Greco to Goya*, National Gallery of Scotland, Edinburgh 1951. — Kunsthalle, Basel 1953 (39 paintings, 144 drawings, 122 prints and 5 tapestries). — *Drawings, Etchings, Lithographs*, The Arts Council, London 1954.

INDEX OF NAMES

Collection of the Count of Romanones: *The Injured Mason* (or *The Building of the Castle*) 36; *The Procession* 36.

New York, Metropolitan Museum of Art: *Majas on a Balcony* 100.

Frick Collection: *The Forge* 112.

Paris, Louvre: *Still Life with a Sheep's Head* 100.

Seville, Cathedral: *Sts Justa and Rufina* 8, 104.

Toledo, Cathedral: *The Betrayal of Christ* 64.

Winterthur, Oskar Reinhart Collection: *Still Life with Salmon* 100.

Tapestry Cartoons:

Madrid, Prado: *The Ball on the Banks of the Manzanares* 20; *The Card Players* 20; *The Crockery Vendor* 20, 22, 24, 25; *The Fair of Madrid* 20, 23; *The Flower-Girls* (or *Spring*) 28, 29, 31; *Picnic on the Grass* 20; *The Sunshade* 20, 21; *The Tobacco Guard* 24, 96; *The Washerwomen* 24, 96.

Portraits:

Amsterdam, Rijksmuseum: *Don Ramón Satue* 9, 112.

Barnard Castle, Bowes Museum (England): *Juan Meléndez Valdés* 65.

Berlin, Kaiser Friedrich Museum: *Don Juan Antonio Llorente* 97.

Bilbao, Felix Valdés Collection: *The Marquis of Santa Cruz* 80; Museum: *Leandro Fernández de Moratín* 9, 122.

Buenos Aires, Jockey Club: *Don Antonio Pórcel* 80.

Cleveland, Museum of Art: *The Architect Don Juan Antonio Cuervo* 8, 112.

Florence, Collection of Prince Ruspoli: *Family of the Infante Don Luis* 27, 68, 69.

London, Otto Beit Collection: *Antonia Zárate* 97.

Wellington Collection: *Portrait of Lord Wellington* 8, 86, 95.

National Gallery: *Doña Isabel Cobos de Pórcel* 74, 80.

Madrid, Royal Academy of History: *Don José de Vargas y Ponce* 80; *King Charles IV and Queen Maria Luisa* 6.

Academy of San Fernando: *Equestrian Portrait of King Ferdinand VII* 8, 87, 88, 95; *Don José Luis de Munárriz* 103; *Leandro Fernández de Moratín* 7, 65; *Don Manuel Godoy* 58, 74; *Self-Portrait* 8, 84, 103; *La Tirana* 44, 96.

Bank of Spain: *Don José de Toro y Zambrano* 6.

Urquijo Bank: *Portrait of the Count of Floridablanca* 6, 14, 27, 31.

Lazaro Museum: *Don Pedro Alcántara de Zúñiga* 5.

Prado: *Portrait of the Duke of Alba* 48, 50; *Doña Tadea Arias de Enríquez* 44; *Francisco Bayeu* 7, 44, 46, 47; *The Family of Charles IV* 7, 28, 58, 68/72; *Equestrian Portrait of King Charles IV* 65; *Equestrian Portrait of Queen Maria Luisa* 65; *Don Isidoro Máiquez* 8, 76, 80, 101; *Don Juan Bautista Muguiro* 9, 122; *The Duke and Duchess of Osuna and their Children* 6, 68; *The Duke of Osuna* 103; *General Don José de Palafox* 95; *General Don Antonio Ricardos* 44; *Self-Portrait* 8, 103; *General Don José de Urrutia* 64.

Royal Palace: *Queen Maria Luisa* 7. Collection of the Duke of Alba: *Duchess of Alba* 3, 4, 7, 44, 47/49, 96.

CONTENTS

On the Jacket:

Portrait of the Count of Fernán-Núñez (detail), *1803.*
Collection of the Duchess of Fernán-Núñez, Madrid.

The Swing (detail), *1787.* Collection of the Duke of Montellano, Madrid.

THIS. VOLUME

THE THIRTEENTH OF THE COLLECTION

THE TASTE OF OUR TIME

WAS PRINTED

BOTH TEXT AND COLORPLATES

BY THE

SKIRA

COLOR STUDIO

AT IMPRIMERIES RÉUNIES S. A., LAUSANNE

FINISHED THE FIFTEENTH DAY OF AUGUST

NINETEEN HUNDRED AND FIFTY-FIVE

THE PLATES WERE ENGRAVED BY

GUEZELLE & RENOUARD, PARIS

*The works reproduced in this volume were photographed
by Hans Hinz, Basel (pages 3, 14, 21, 22, 23, 25, 29, 30, 33, 34, 35, 36, 41, 45, 56, 60, 61, 63, 75, 91,
92, 93, 98, 99, 107, 108, 109, 111, 112, 113, 114, 115, 117, 118, 121),
by Louis Laniepce, Paris (page 66),
by Henry B. Beville, Washington (page 10),
by courtesy of the magazine Du, Zurich (pages 43, 46, 67, 76, 81, 82, 84, 96)
and by courtesy of the Art Institute of Chicago (Richard J. Brittain, photographer) (pages 78 and 79).*

PRINTED IN SWITZERLAND